BERKSHIRE, BUCKINGHAMSHIRE AND OXFORDSHIRE

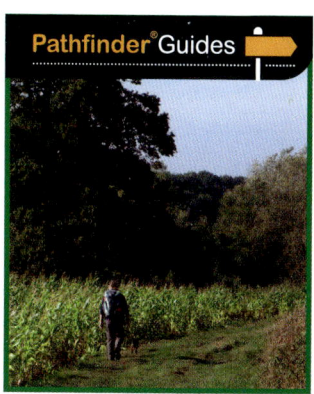

Outstanding Circular Walks

Compiled by Vivienne Crow

Contents			Short walks up to 2½ hours	11
At-a-glance		2	Slightly harder walks of 3–3½ hours	37
Keymap		4	Longer walks of more than 3½ hours	68
Introduction		5	Further Information	92

At-a-glance

Walk		Page	🥾	🏁	🚏	⛰	🕐
1	Broughton Castle	12	Broughton Castle	SP 419 382	2¾ miles (4.4km)	270ft (80m)	1¼ hrs
2	Shotover	14	Shotover Country Park	SP 563 062	2¾ miles (4.4km)	280ft (85m)	1¼ hrs
3	Burnham Beeches	16	Burnham Beeches	SU 957 850	3¼ miles (5.2km)	200ft (60m)	1½ hrs
4	Farmoor Reservoir and the River Thames	18	Farmoor Reservoir	SP 452 060	3¾ miles (6km)	120ft (35m)	1¾ hrs
5	Leygrove's Wood	20	Cadmore End	SU 784 927	3¾ miles (6.1km)	390ft (120m)	2 hrs
6	Aston Rowant National Nature Reserve	22	Aston Rowant NNR	SU 734 967	4 miles (6.4km)	515ft (155m)	2 hrs
7	Stowe Park	24	Chackmore	SP 683 357	4¼ miles (6.8km)	290ft (90m)	2 hrs
8	Walbury Hill	26	Walbury Hill	SU 369 620	4½ miles (7.4km)	575ft (175m)	2¼ hrs
9	Brill	28	Brill	SP 652 141	4¾ miles (7.7km)	460ft (140m)	2½ hrs
10	Greenham Common and the Kennet & Avon Canal	30	Greenham Common	SU 499 651	5 miles (8.1km)	200ft (60m)	2½ hrs
11	Hurley, Ashley Hill and the River Thames	32	Hurley	SU 825 840	5¼ miles (8.5km)	425ft (130m)	2½ hrs
12	River Thames at Shiplake	34	Shiplake Station	SU 776 797	5½ miles (9km)	170ft (50m)	2½ hrs
13	Milton-under-Wychwood and Bruern Abbey	38	Milton-under-Wychwood	SP 264 183	6 miles (9.7km)	320ft (100m)	3 hrs
14	Pishill and Stonor Park	41	Pishill	SU 726 898	6 miles (9.7km)	795ft (240m)	3 hrs
15	Windsor Great Park and Virginia Water	44	Virginia Water	SU 960 687	6 miles (9.8km)	360ft (110m)	3 hrs
16	Devil's Punchbowl	47	Sparsholt Firs	SU 343 850	6½ miles (10.4km)	375ft (115m)	3 hrs
17	Claydon House	50	Claydon House	SP 718 249	6½ miles (10.6km)	285ft (85m)	3 hrs
18	Bucklebury Common	53	Bucklebury Common	SU 560 692	6½ miles (10.6km)	300ft (90m)	3 hrs
19	Badbury Hill and Great Coxwell	56	Badbury Hill	SU 261 945	6½ miles (10.6km)	510ft (155m)	3 hrs
20	Deddington and the Oxford Canal	59	Deddington	SP 467 316	8 miles (12.9km)	270ft (80m)	3½ hrs
21	Waddesdon	62	Waddesdon	SP 749 168	7 miles (11.3km)	310ft (95m)	3¼ hrs
22	Wendover Woods	65	Wendover Woods	SP 889 089	6¾ miles (11km)	920ft (280m)	3½ hrs
23	Ridgeway and West Ilsley	69	Bury Down	SU 479 840	7¾ miles (12.4km)	510ft (155m)	3¾ hrs
24	Chalgrove	72	Chalgrove	SU 636 968	8 miles (12.9km)	325ft (100m)	3¾ hrs
25	Lambourn Downs	76	Lambourn	SU 325 788	8¾ miles (14.2km)	570ft (175m)	4¼ hrs
26	Uffington White Horse and Wayland's Smithy	80	Whitehorse Hill, Uffington	SU 293 865	8¾ miles (14.2km)	720ft (220m)	4¼ hrs
27	River Lambourn and Donnington Castle	84	Snelsmore Common	SU 463 710	9½ miles (15.3km)	530ft (160m)	4½ hrs
28	Blenheim and beyond	88	Woodstock	SP 447 167	10¼ miles (16.6km)	700ft (215m)	5 hrs

Comments

A pleasant walk over farmland from Broughton Castle. Keep your camera handy on the return leg through the parkland, for tree-framed views of the grand manor house.
This short walk on the edge of Oxford is a circuit of part of a country park, formerly a royal hunting forest, with tantalising glimpses of the distant hills.
An easy-going short walk on surfaced forest trails around the historic and delightfully atmospheric woodland-pasture not far from the edge of London.
A lesser-walked reservoir circuit combined with a lovely rural stretch of the Thames Path, where birdsong trills from the hedgerows.
Taking to the woodlands and open, undulating farmland north of Cadmore End, watch the sky for red kites on this walk as they are never far away.
Sample an unbeatable combination of sumptuous ancient woodland and pristine chalk grassland on this walk with far-reaching views across the Oxford plain from Beacon Hill.
An inviting circuit around the National Trust parkland at Stowe that is gradually being restored to its former 18th-century glory, when it was one of the finest in England.
Beginning from Walbury Hill, the highest point in South East England, this short walk calls in at Combe, a delightful hamlet hidden in the folds of the hills.
Breathtaking views, a 17th-century windmill and a duck decoy are just three of the intriguing ingredients in this magical little walk from Brill.
Once the site of a major airbase and a peace camp, this walk combines a visit to Berkshire's largest area of heathland with a ramble beside the beautiful Kennet & Avon Canal.
Setting out from the attractive and historic village of Hurley, this walk climbs to Ashley Hill and returns alongside a particularly gorgeous section of the River Thames from Frogmill.
Following the River Thames upstream from Shiplake Station, this route explores the elegant countryside between Reading and Henley-on-Thames.
An enchanting outing in the Evenlode valley in the Oxfordshire Cotswolds, passing through Foxholes Nature Reserve and the attractive village of Fifield.
Having enjoyable and ever-changing views, this ramble is set in the beguiling countryside of the Chilterns and meanders through the undulating deer park at Stonor.
Taking to the shore path around tranquil Virginia Water, this walk goes on to roam through the woodlands, lawns and gardens of a small corner of Windsor Great Park.
The views on this walk along part of the Ridgeway on the northern edge of the North Wessex Downs seem to go on forever.
This easy-going walk culminates in a visit to Claydon House, where Florence Nightingale spent several summers, and passes through two charming villages featuring in the Domesday Book.
This figure-of-eight walk tours the woodlands and heathland to the north of Thatcham. A route to savour on a summer evening when nightjars may be heard on the heath.
Highlights of this walk include Great Coxwell, with its impressive tithe barn, picturesque cottages and ancient church, plus the distant views to the North Wessex Downs and Uffington White Horse.
From the medieval market town of Deddington, this is a circuit of the very pleasant north Oxfordshire countryside south of Banbury, including a section of Oxford Canal towpath.
The Buckinghamshire village of Waddesdon is dominated by the presence of its château-like Manor that hides in the woodland above. This walk completes a circuit of the hill on which it sits.
The Chilterns is noted for its fine deciduous woodland, and one of the best places to experience it is on this walk through the sprawling forest of Wendover Woods.
Bookended by sections along the Ridgeway National Trail, this circular from Bury Down showcases the variety of North Wessex Downs scenery and calls in at idyllic West Ilsley.
A walk of graceful churches and welcoming pubs, visiting Chalgrove, the historic hamlet of Newington, tranquil Berrick Prior and a return via pretty Brightwell Baldwin.
There's a wonderful sense of expansiveness as you stride out along the ridge-tops, with big skies dominating these wide, open spaces on this Berkshire Downs walk.
There's a strong sense of stepping back in time on this route, our ancestors having left their mark: the White Horse, the hillfort of Uffington Castle and Wayland's Smithy.
A Lambourn valley ramble along woodland trails, good tracks, quiet lanes and riverside paths in a circular walk from Snelsmore Common, passing Donnington Castle.
In addition to handsome Georgian Woodstock and views of Blenheim Palace from the rolling parkland paths, this walk partly follows a Roman road and visits North Leigh Roman villa.

Keymap

Introduction to Berkshire, Buckinghamshire and Oxfordshire

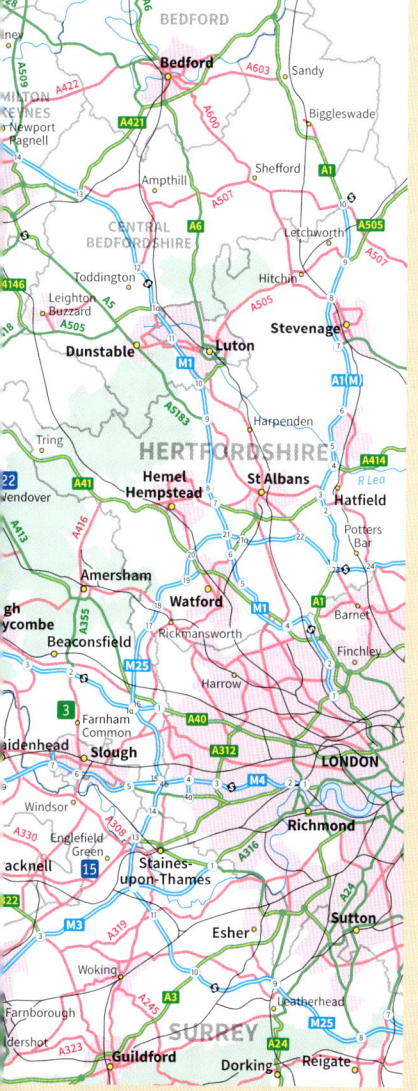

This title fills a gap in the coverage of the Pathfinder series between PF (06) Cotswolds and PF (25) Thames Valley and Chilterns, particularly in the region covered by the south-central Midlands. From the beech and bluebell woods of the Chilterns to the chalk uplands of the North Wessex Downs; and from the tranquil meanders of the River Thames to the honey-coloured cottages of the Cotswold villages, the ceremonial counties of Berkshire, Buckinghamshire and Oxfordshire have a lot to offer walkers. They cover an area that stretches from Sandhurst in the south – on the Surrey and Hampshire borders – all the way up to Banbury in the north – just a stone's throw from Northamptonshire. With a population of more than two million people and encompassing some busy towns along the western edge of London, it's still easy to escape the crowds; to find hidden woods, tranquil riverside trails and airy chalk ridges where you'll hardly see a soul.

There are three National Landscapes (formerly Areas of Outstanding Natural Beauty – AONBs) within the three counties – the Chilterns, the North Wessex Downs and the Cotswolds – each with its own character. If it's woodland you're after, head for the Chilterns.

A junction of paths on Walbury Hill, Berkshire (Walk 8)

This line of chalk hills stretches from central Bedfordshire in the north-east to the River Thames in the south-west. Although there are cultivated downs and areas of open grassland within the National Landscape, it is best known for its woods. The towering beech trees put on a magnificent display in the autumn and winter when the canopy, followed by the woodland floor, turns a coppery colour, but spring and summer have their delights too when bluebells and leaves full of youth and vigour bring energy back to these forests. The western escarpment is punctuated by several impressive viewpoints, including Wendover's Aston Hill and Stokenchurch's Beacon Hill, looking out over the vales of Aylesbury and Oxford.

Although an extension of the same line of chalk hills as the Chilterns, the North Wessex Downs are a different beast entirely. This is where walkers come to stride out on long ridge lines and enjoy the rich variety of wildflowers, birds and insects found on the open grassland. While combes, or dry valleys, cut into the softly rolling landscape, easy-going chalk tracks, some used for millennia, make their way between fields of golden crops and the sumptuous green of the horseracing gallops. The National Landscape itself covers parts of Oxfordshire, Berkshire, Wiltshire and Hampshire, and has a palpable sense of antiquity that's unrivalled in this

part of England. There are hundreds of prehistoric sites, ranging from the well known and easily identifiable – Uffington White Horse, Wayland's Smithy long barrow and Badbury Hill among them – to the enigmatic, often unnamed earthworks that rise like a rash of pimples from the fields.

The third National Landscape, and the largest in the country, is the Cotswolds. Generally associated with Gloucestershire, it also covers parts of five other counties, most notably west Oxfordshire. A handful of the walks in this book start in or close to the National Landscape, an area characterised by idyllic villages straddling crystal-clear streams and surrounded by low, limestone hills that are home to beech woods and rare grassland habitats.

In between these protected landscapes, there are many fascinating features, both natural and of human construct, as well as pockets of exceptional beauty. The River Thames, for example, carves its way through a varied and delightful valley, all the way from its upper reaches in the meadows bordering the Cotswolds through Oxford, Goring and Marlow to London's westernmost suburbs. There are public rights of way along at least one bank for most of its length, with the Thames Path National Trail providing a well-waymarked route. Other rivers include the Thame, Evenlode, Windrush, Cherwell, Lambourn and Kennet, while towpaths enable walkers to keep gentle pace with colourful narrowboats on some of the region's man-made waterways. The Grand Union, Oxford and the Kennet & Avon are the three main canals that pass through the area.

The presence of rivers, different woodland types and a wide variety of other habitats means there is always a good chance of coming across wildlife while exploring the countryside. The Berkshire, Buckinghamshire and Oxfordshire Wildlife Trust manages a number of reserves throughout the three counties, including Greenham and Crookham Commons near Newbury and Snelsmore Common Country Park near Donnington. In addition, there are several National Nature Reserves, protected for their important wildlife species or geology. Aston Rowant and Burnham Beeches are examples – and feature on walks in this book.

One of most exciting bird species is the red kite. It's also one that you're almost guaranteed to see. With this striking, fork-tailed bird of prey extinct in England and Scotland, and numbers threatened on a global scale, a decision was made in the 1980s to begin an ambitious reintroduction programme. Some of the first bird releases took place in the Chilterns in 1989 and they have been breeding successfully ever since. The RSPB estimates there are now more than 4,000 breeding pairs in Britain.

Owing largely to the proximity of London and the attractiveness of the surrounding countryside, Berkshire, Buckinghamshire and Oxfordshire all have more than their share of stately homes and large country estates. Let's not forget that Berkshire is the county that gave us the ultimate in 'stately', albeit in the form of a royal residence – Windsor Castle. Blenheim Palace, Waddesdon Manor and Stowe, are among the biggest and best known in the region. Many of these properties, as well as some slightly humbler homes, have strong links with historic figures. Blenheim, for example, is where Winston Churchill was born, while Florence Nightingale had rooms at her sister's Buckinghamshire home, Claydon House.

The physical character of the region's settlements depends largely on local factors, most notably geology. Everyone is familiar with the rich, almost golden-coloured oolitic limestone of the Cotswold villages and market towns – it is one of the features that draw so many visitors into the National Landscape – but buildings differ throughout the three counties. In Berkshire, for example, you're more likely to see churches, farms and cottages incorporating flint.

Great Coxwell Barn, Oxfordshire (Walk 19)

Cruising on the Oxford Canal, Oxfordshire (Walk 20)

Also, because of the paucity of local stone, there are more timber-framed buildings. The latter is also true of Buckinghamshire, although brick began to appear from the 16th century onwards. Partly a reflection of the larger area covered by the county, Oxfordshire's historic buildings use a much wider range of materials, including several types of limestone.

Thatched roofing is a common feature of many cottages throughout the area, increasingly so as large numbers of people want their rural homes to have a more rustic or 'natural' appearance. The traditional thatching in this part of the UK, using straw, features large overhangs and a curved shape. The result is rather pleasing to the eye, giving even the most ordinary of villages a sense of being unspoiled.

It's hardly surprising then that Berkshire, Buckinghamshire and Oxfordshire are popular with walkers. Two National Trails pass through the region – the Thames Path and the Ridgeway. These waymarked, long-distance paths are funded by Natural England and maintained by local authorities. Several of the walks in this book use sections of them. Watch for the acorn symbol that acts as a guide on all National Trails in England and Wales.

In addition to these routes, there are dozens of other long-distance paths criss-crossing the area. Some are well waymarked, some aren't; some are well maintained, some seem to have been forgotten by the bodies that established them. Among the many that people will encounter while walking the routes in this book are the Test Way, the Lambourn Valley Way, the Chiltern Way, Shakespeare's Way, the Oxford Greenbelt Way, the Oxfordshire Way and Hampshire County Council's Wayfarer's Walk. Like the National Trails, these 'recreational paths' are identified by lines of green diamonds on Ordnance Survey's 1:25,000 Explorer maps or pink diamonds on the 1:50,000 Landranger maps.

Even beyond the long-distance paths, waymarking and general path maintenance are usually of a relatively high standard. Of course, there are paths that become muddy after a week of autumn downpours, and there are a few, less well-walked trails that can become overgrown in the height of summer, but paths and path furniture (stiles, gates and bridges) tend to be kept in good repair, making for a pleasant experience. For this, we have to thank local authorities' increasingly hard-pressed countryside access officers, National Trust rangers and the growing bands of volunteers who regularly go out into the countryside with their tools and their enthusiasm to cut back brambles, fix stiles, remove fallen trees and erect signposts. Each of the National Trails has a volunteer scheme; the National Trust organises its own conservation teams; the work of the ever-busy Chiltern Society is always noticeable; and local Ramblers' groups sometimes get involved. In the Chilterns, white arrows on tree trunks, in particular, prove to be invaluable navigational aids in autumn and winter when leaves obscure the trails through the National Landscape's woods.

Beautiful landscapes, an excellent path network, attractive towns and villages, wildlife-rich habitats, locations that are far from the madding crowd and fascinating historical features at every twist and turn of the trail... There's everything here that a lowland walker could want. What are you waiting for? Let's go!

> This book includes a list of waypoints alongside the description of the walk, so that you can enjoy the full benefits of gps should you wish to. For more information about route navigation, improving your map reading ability, walking with a GPS and for an introduction to basic map and compass techniques, read Pathfinder® Guide *Navigation Skills for Walkers* by outdoor writer Terry Marsh (ISBN 978-0-319-09175-3). This title is available in bookshops and online at shop.ordnancesurvey.co.uk

Beech woods to the north of Cadmore End

Short walks up to 2½ hours

walk 1

Broughton Castle

Start
Broughton Castle, Oxfordshire, 2 miles (3.2km) south-west of Banbury on the B4035

Distance
2¾ miles (4.4km)

Height gain
270 feet (80m)

Approximate time
1¼ hours

Route terrain
Open parkland; field paths; tracks

Parking
Small layby on southbound side of B4053, 230 yards south of the crossroads in Broughton

Dog friendly
One awkward stile where dogs may need lifting **A**

OS maps
Landranger 151 (Stratford-upon-Avon); Explorer 191 (Banbury, Bicester & Chipping Norton)

GPS waypoints
- SP 419 382
- **A** SP 416 387
- **B** SP 418 397
- **C** SP 412 388

A wander through the pretty parkland next to Broughton Castle is followed by a short walk across farmland to the edge of North Newington. The route back leads over a small hilltop with good views of the surrounding countryside. Keep your camera handy on the return leg through the parkland, where tree-framed views of the grand manor house come and go.

From the layby, cross the B4053 and drop down the grass verge opposite to join a walled path to the church. Walk through the churchyard, exiting via a gate on the far side. Follow the surfaced lane away from the castle for less than 100 yards. As it bends right, continue heading north-north-west up through the open parkland. There is no path on the ground and no waymarkers to act as a guide. After 450 yards on this trajectory though, a stile should be reached in a fence **A**. (This is about 90 yards to the left of a pair of gates.) Cross the stile, turn right along the road and take the next lane on the left.

Drawing level with a cottage on the right, turn left through a gap in the hedge. A path heads roughly north through the middle of the field. In the far right-hand corner (out of sight initially), go through another hedge gap and then veer slightly right to walk beside the hedgerow on the right. At the top of the rise, keep straight ahead, walking between high hedges. Go through a pair of gates and continue north on a faint, grassy trail that dips, climbs and dips again to reach a kissing-gate. Beyond this, continue straight on, aiming for a large gate. There's a metal kissing-gate just to the right of this. Go through and turn left (straight on for the **Blinking Owl** pub) along the path on the edge of North Newington. Just after a cottage on the right, head up the short tree-covered embankment on the left **B**.

Walk through the middle of the field (south-west), rising gently at first. On the far side, go through the hedge gap and turn left. About 45 yards beyond where the hedgerow on the left ends, a new field is entered. Bear right, heading south-west again and climbing. In the top corner of the field, go through the small wooden gate in the hedgerow on the right and then bear left along the field edge. This small hill provides some lovely views of the surrounding countryside, with woods and fields leading off into the distance. Bear left after the next gate, down the field edge.

The moated manor house of Broughton Castle

Broughton Castle

This moated manor house was built in 1306, with castle-like embellishments added in the 15th century. During the English Civil War, Royalists laid siege to the site, causing considerable damage. Today, it is the home of the Fiennes family who have owned it since 1447. The public are admitted on open days.

Turn left at a lane ❻ and immediately right along a rough track. Reaching an open-sided barn, turn sharp left (east-south-east) across the field. Broughton Castle's parkland is re-entered at the next gate. With no guiding paths or waymarkers, walk with the trees on the right at first. Then, on the far side of this small copse, swing slightly left (east-north-east), soon looking down on Broughton Castle. After 275 yards on this line, rejoin the outward route by heading down to the right (south-south-east). Drop to the track and follow it back to the church. Retrace steps to where the walk started.

BROUGHTON CASTLE ● 13

walk 2

Shotover

Start
Shotover, Oxfordshire, 3 miles (4.8km) east of Oxford city centre

Distance
2¾ miles (4.4km)

Height gain
280 feet (85m)

Approximate time
1¼ hours

Route terrain
Rough tracks; pavement through village; woodland

Parking
Shotover Country Park car park at eastern end of Old Road, Headington

Dog friendly
This is a dog-friendly walk

OS maps
Landranger 164 (Oxford), Explorer 180 (Oxford)

GPS waypoints
- SP 563 062
- Ⓐ SP 575 058
- Ⓑ SP 569 050
- Ⓒ SP 561 056
- Ⓓ SP 563 059

Located on the eastern edge of the city of Oxford, Shotover Country Park once formed part of a royal hunting forest but is now popular as a destination for walkers, cyclists and horse riders. This short walk circuits part of the park, enjoying occasional glimpses of distant hills along the way.

With your back to the lane leading into the car park, walk to the opposite corner and join a rough track, a restricted byway, heading roughly east. Immediately after passing the gates to a reservoir compound, take the track on the right Ⓐ.

Miles of trails criss-cross Shotover Country Park

Shotover Country Park

Oxford City Council has managed the woods, meadows and heathland here since the 1930s. During World War Two, Shotover Hill was used for military training and for testing tanks built at nearby Cowley. The site is now home to a range of wildlife, including green woodpeckers, willow warblers, roe deer and white admiral butterflies.

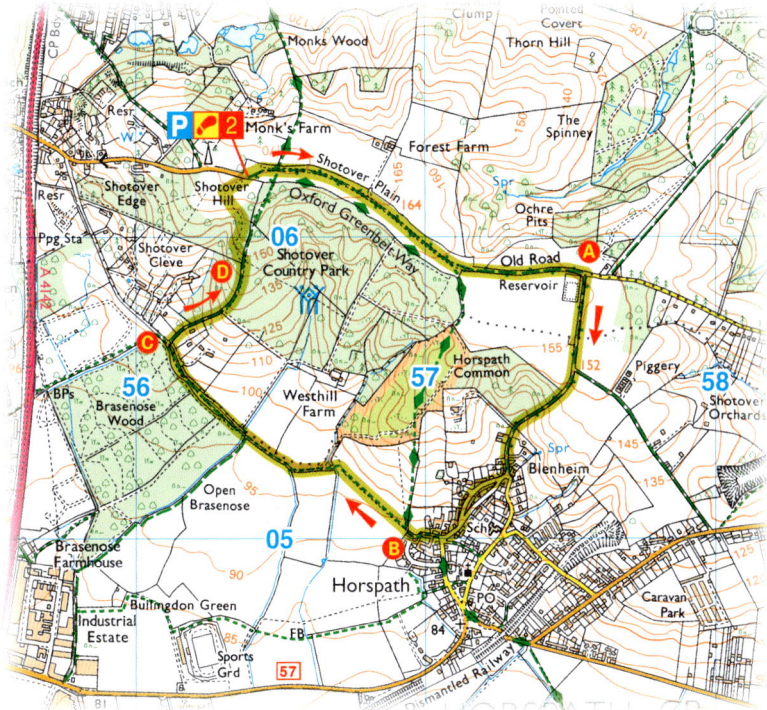

Keep straight on as another track goes left and descend through pretty woodland to the village of Blenheim. With a thatched cottage on the right, turn right along Spring Lane. When this starts descending, there's a view across the top of the Mini car plant at Cowley to the North Wessex Downs in the distance.

When Spring Lane meets Manor Farm Road, keep right along the walkway, crossing the entrance to the Tuso site to follow an enclosed path. Bear right when this splits and then go through a kissing-gate **B**. A faint trail heads straight across the field. On the far side, go through the kissing-gate in the hedgerow to the left. Once back out in the open, keep to the left-hand edge of two fields, separated by a strip of trees. Reaching Brasenose Wood, there's a confusing array of paths; keep straight on, along a partially surfaced track for 450 yards and then pass around the side of the barriers on the right. Ignoring the gates over to the left, keep straight ahead on a shady path **C** that soon begins climbing.

At a crossing of paths at the top of the initial rise, turn left, ascending more gently now. Go straight over another path crossing but then, in 100 yards, take the trail on the left. This quickly splits twice. At the first fork, keep left and, at the second, bear right **D**. There's one last taste of these lovely woods before emerging in an open area. Keep right, walking just to the left of the trees and brambles, for another 50 yards or so and then stroll across the grass to the noticeboards on the far side. In doing so, turn round for a lovely glimpse of the tree-topped hills on the far side of Oxford. Go through the gate to return to the parking area. ●

walk 3

Burnham Beeches

Start
Burnham Beeches, Buckinghamshire, about 2 miles (3km) north of Slough

Distance
3¼ miles (5.2km)

Height gain
200 feet (60m)

Approximate time
1½ hours

Route terrain
Asphalt drives and woodland trails

Parking
Lord Mayor's Drive car park at Burnham Beeches

Dog friendly
Yes, but dogs must be on leads in some areas

OS maps
Landranger 175 (Reading & Windsor), Explorer 172 (Chiltern Hills East)

GPS waypoints
- SU 957 850
- Ⓐ SU 946 845
- Ⓑ SU 940 849
- Ⓒ SU 946 855
- Ⓓ SU 957 858

Using easy-going surfaced drives and forest trails, this short walk samples the delights of atmospheric wood-pasture on the edge of London. Many of the ancient beech and oak trees of Burnham Beeches have been pollarded for centuries – cut to just above head height every 10 to 15 years to provide firewood. The woods are also home to several important archaeological sites.

> **Burnham Beeches** This ancient wood-pasture was bought by the Corporation of London in 1880 to save it from development, and the City still owns and manages it today. The trees owe their longevity to pollarding, with their holes and deadwood now home to a range of birds, plants, fungi and invertebrates. Livestock would have grazed the site for centuries, and cattle, pigs and Exmoor ponies have recently been reintroduced to encourage habitat diversity.

 From the parking area, continue following Lord Mayor's Drive (also known as Beeches Way) west into the heart of the woods. Soon after the **Beeches Eco Café**, bear left when the lane forks. Keep straight ahead, through the gate.

Later pass the 800-year-old Druids' Oak, protected by a fence. On the opposite side of the drive is the Seven Way Plain fort, thought to date from the early Iron Age.

Turn right after the next set of gates Ⓐ, passing to the right of a sheltered seating area. The path runs to the left of a fence. Drawing level with a large gate in this fence (about 200 yards beyond the shelter), bear left, walking downhill. At a crossing of paths, go straight over, climbing out of the dip on a trail that is hard to make out when covered by autumn leaves. Keep to the clearest path as it makes its way to a road junction Ⓑ.

Turn right along Park Lane. After 600 yards on the asphalt, there is a green barrier on the right near a Corporation of London sign. (This is the second barrier on the right.) Turn right here to follow Morton Drive back into the woods proper. Continue past a set of green bollards. Then, immediately after passing a small timber shelter, bear left as the way ahead splits Ⓒ. Now on McAuliffe Drive, soon see the overgrown earthworks and flooded ditch of Hartley Court, a medieval defended settlement, on the left.

Turn left at a junction near another large Corporation of London sign. This is Duke's Drive. About 70 yards short of a metal barrier across the track, take the woodland trail on the right Ⓓ. Partly obscured by fallen leaves in autumn, this winds

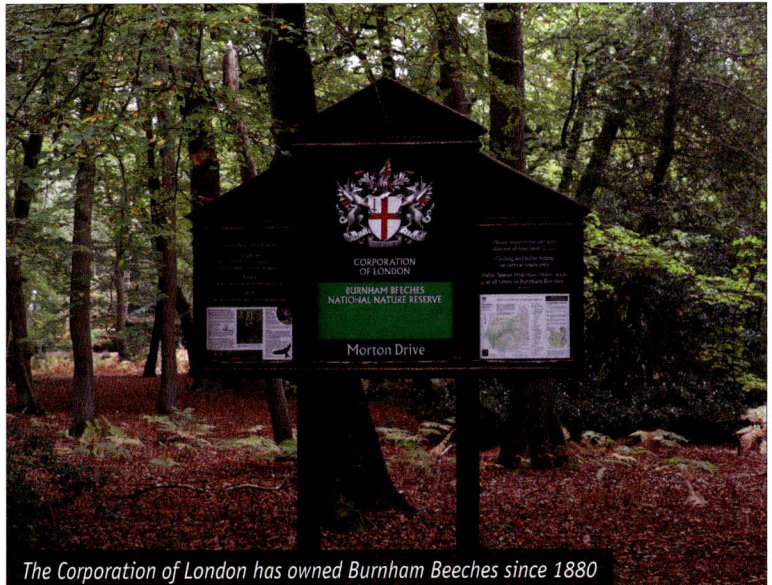

The Corporation of London has owned Burnham Beeches since 1880

its way through the trees, staying roughly parallel with a road to the left. The general direction is south-south-west. Turn left at a T-junction and then take the next path on the right. (If you reach the road, you've overshot the right turn by about 100 yards.) The path dips to cross a small bridge in a particularly atmospheric part of the woods and then climbs again. It emerges from the trees on the surfaced lane opposite the parking area where the walk started.

0 200 400 600 800 METRES 1 KILOMETRES
0 200 400 600 YARDS ½ MILES

SCALE 1:25 000 or 2½ INCHES to 1 MILE 4CM to 1KM

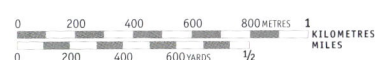

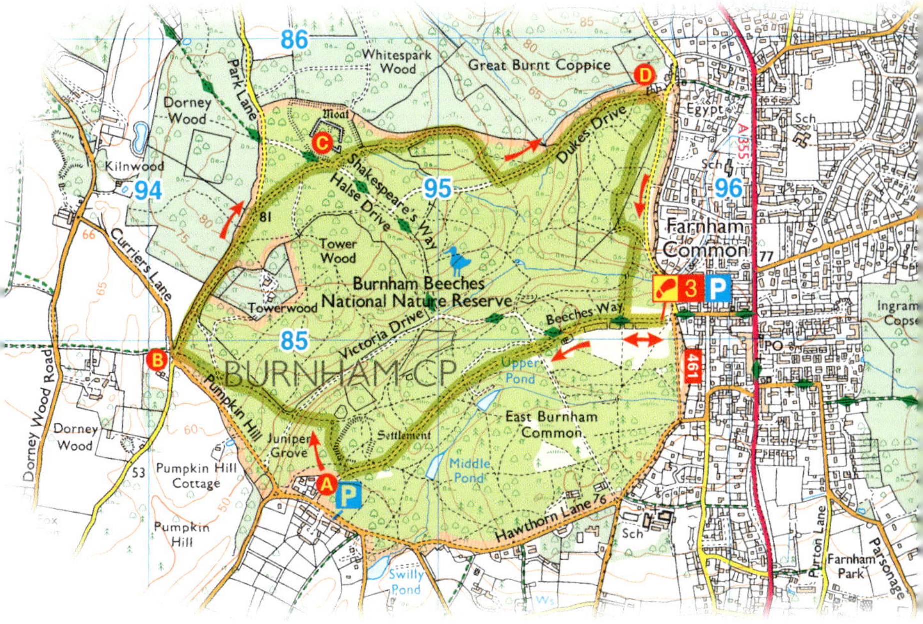

walk 4

Farmoor Reservoir and the River Thames

Start
Farmoor Reservoir, Oxfordshire, 3 miles (4.8km) south of Eynsham

Distance
3¾ miles (6km)

Height gain
120 feet (35m)

Approximate time
1¾ hours

Route terrain
Nature trail; quiet lane; riverside path

Parking
Farmoor Reservoir car park

Dog friendly
Yes. (This walk avoids the reservoir path itself where a dog ban is in force)

OS maps
Landranger 164 (Oxford), Explorer 180 (Oxford)

GPS waypoints
SP 452 060
A SP 450 053
B SP 439 055
C SP 441 069
D SP 445 071
E SP 451 066

Many walkers who visit Farmoor Reservoir keep to the main path along the water's edge, but they're missing out... Encircling this circuit is a far more interesting route that, as well as making use of the waymarked 'Countryside Walk', takes in a delightful section of the River Thames. There's a good chance of spotting wildlife, and you don't have to be an ornithologist to appreciate the beautiful concerts performed by the warblers and other birds in Buckthorn Meadow in the summer.

Standing in the car park with your back to the reservoir, look to the right to locate a small toilet block. Walk over to this and then join the constructed path to the left of it. This is part of the waymarked 'Countryside Walk' which is followed for much of this route. After another toilet block (on the left), bear right along a field edge. Soon the reservoir appears which is popular with water sports enthusiasts. About ½ mile (800m) beyond the car park, the signposted route bends sharp left and joins a lane **A**. Turn right here. Having walked the asphalt for 400 yards, take the boardwalk on the right. When this ends, keep forward on a fenced path. After a bridge, turn right along the lane. Take the footpath to the left of a large gate. This leads to the banks of the River Thames **B**. Turn right, heading downstream.

The path never strays far from the water's edge for the next 1¼ miles (2km), although the meandering river isn't always in sight. It passes through Buckthorn Meadow along the way where with luck it should be possible to hear or even see various warblers during the summer. Bear left on reaching a surfaced path. After a bridge over a reservoir channel, bear left along a grassy riverside path. Just after passing the Farmoor Gauging Station on the right, the path bends sharp right. Keep right at the next trail junction and soon return to the riverbank proper again. Keep left as a path joins from the right. Then, at a fingerpost **C**, keep straight on, parting company with the Thames.

Go straight across a surfaced lane. After ignoring an unmarked turning to the left, walk to the right of a narrow band of trees. Keeping right, later reach another constructed

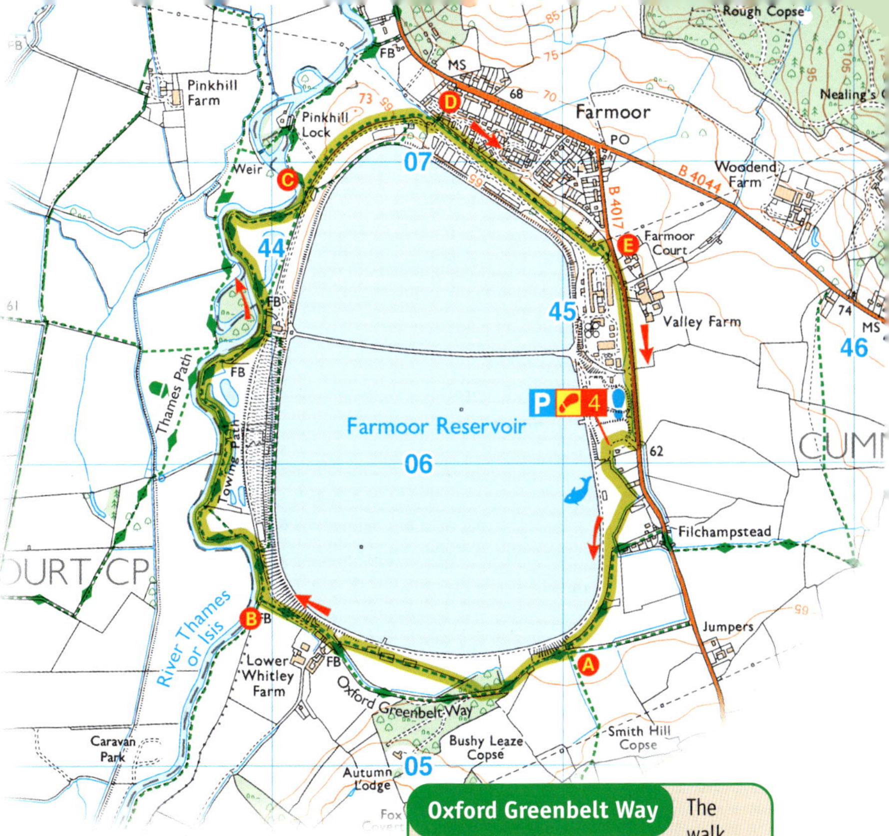

0 200 400 600 800 METRES 1 KILOMETRES
MILES
0 200 400 600 YARDS ½

SCALE 1:25 000 or 2½ INCHES to 1 MILE *4CM to 1KM*

path. Turn left along this. Go left again at a track junction and, almost immediately, take the path on the right **D**, walking beside metal railings. Emerging from the most overgrown part of the path, walk beside a green-fenced compound. Follow this boundary round to the left and then turn right along a surfaced track.

Go through the gate near the road and then pick up the continuing 'Countryside Walk' on the far side of the water treatment works' access lane **E**. The trail runs parallel with the B4017 for the next ⅓ mile (600m). It crosses straight over another Thames Water access point. The next time asphalt is encountered is at the entrance to the reservoir car park. Turn right to re-enter the parking area. ●

Oxford Greenbelt Way The walk coincides with the Oxford Greenbelt Way around the south and west of Farmoor Reservoir. This 50-mile (80-km) long-distance path was devised by the environmental campaigning charity, the CPRE, in 2007 to highlight the importance of England's Green Belts.

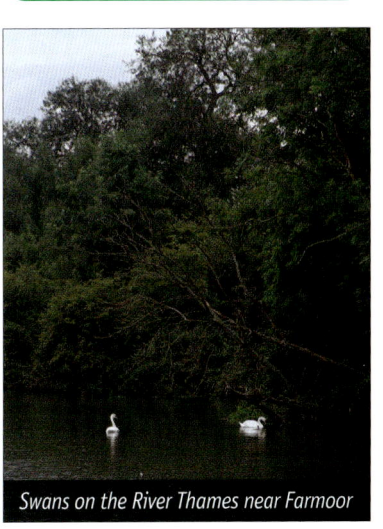

Swans on the River Thames near Farmoor

walk 5

Leygrove's Wood

Start
Cadmore End, Buckinghamshire

Distance
3¾ miles (6.1km)

Height gain
390 feet (120m)

Approximate time
2 hours

Route terrain
Tracks; woodland paths; fields

Parking
Small Forestry England parking area at entrance to Leygrove's Wood

Dog friendly
This is a dog-friendly walk

OS maps
Landranger 175 (Reading & Windsor), Explorer 171 (Chiltern Hills West)

GPS waypoints
- SU 784 927
- Ⓐ SU 787 931
- Ⓑ SU 785 942
- Ⓒ SU 791 943
- Ⓓ SU 799 943
- Ⓔ SU 791 935

This lovely stroll weaves its way through woods and across rolling farmland to the north of Cadmore End. There's a good chance of spotting a variety of wildlife among the different tree types, including deer, the ubiquitous squirrel and a range of bird species. As ever, watch the sky for red kites – they're never far away in this part of the country.

Follow the track on the far side of the barrier. About 100 yards after it passes under the motorway, bear right along a trail through Pound Wood. When this drops on to a track, turn right, soon crossing a neck of open land. About 40 yards after re-entering the trees at a barrier, turn left up a rising track Ⓐ. This is the start of the loop section of the walk; the route returns to this point later.

Cross a track junction and take the narrow trail opposite. Go straight over a grass track and climb back out into the open. Keep straight ahead, walking uphill with a hedgerow on the right. On the far side of the field, turn left and then follow a track round to the right, past Dell's Farm. Go through the kissing-gate on the far side of the farm's access lane Ⓑ and veer slightly right to enter Dell's Wood via a pedestrian gate. A trail winds its way between the glorious beech trees, with navigation aided by occasional white arrows painted on their trunks. These waymarkers become more important after a

An uncultivated strip between fields fringed by woodland

> ### The hermit of Cadmore End
>
> Jack Butler lived in Pound Wood from the middle of World War One until he died, aged 88, in 1936. His home was a shack made of branches and tin sheets, and his only income came from doing odd jobs and selling bundles of firewood. He told locals that he was a prophet and he seemed convinced he would never die.

kissing-gate when the route swings slightly right of its previous line.

Dropping to a clearer path, turn right. Leave the woods via a gate next to a barrier **C** and keep straight ahead on a grass strip between fields fringed to the north by more woodland. On reaching a rough track, turn right. Just before the next field, turn right through a gap in the hedges **D** and enter a narrow strip of trees at a waymarker post. Keep left, along the clearer route, when the path forks.

Entering Barn Wood at a fence, ignore the arrow showing a trail to the left; instead, keep straight on. Cross a rough track and walk round the side of the barrier to join a forest track, along which bear left **E**. This leads back to the barrier just beyond **A**. Now retrace steps from the outward leg, remembering to turn left up the trail through the trees at the next waymarker post and then follow the track back to the car park.

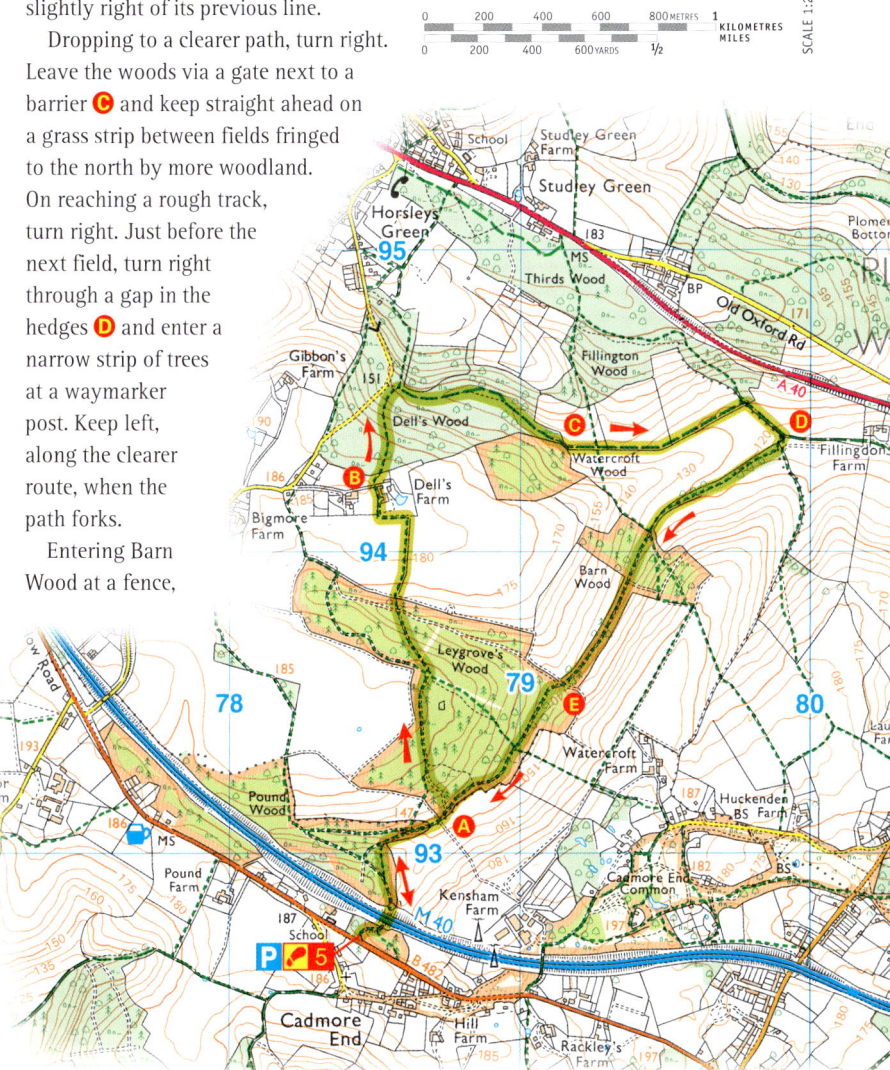

LEYGROVE'S WOOD ● 21

walk 6

Aston Rowant National Nature Reserve

Start
Aston Rowant National Nature Reserve, Buckinghamshire, 2 miles (3km) west of Stokenchurch

Distance
4 miles (6.4km)

Height gain
515 feet (155m)

Approximate time
2 hours

Route terrain
Woodland paths; chalk grassland; farmland; short section beside road

Parking
Aston Rowant National Nature Reserve's Cherry Tree Corner car park

Dog friendly
This is a dog-friendly walk

OS maps
Landranger 165 (Aylesbury & Leighton Buzzard), Explorer 171 (Chiltern Hills West)

GPS waypoints
SU 734 967
Ⓐ SU 728 971
Ⓑ SU 726 968
Ⓒ SU 723 973
Ⓓ SU 734 981
Ⓔ SU 737 976
Ⓕ SU 744 972

The woods in and around the Aston Rowant National Nature Reserve are an absolute delight at any time of the year – green and sumptuous in spring and summer; sparkling with colour on sunny autumn days; and truly atmospheric in winter. This route has the added bonus of crossing the open chalk grassland of Beacon Hill, with its far-reaching views over the Oxford plain to the west. All the while, walkers follow in ancient footsteps, making use of a disused turnpike road and the Icknield Way, one of the oldest routeways in the UK, thought to predate the Romans.

Enter the woods at the information panels and keep left, ignoring the signposted path to the right. Bear left at a waymarked fork. Leaving the woods via a gate Ⓐ, head out on to Beacon Hill. The chalk grasslands here are home to several species of orchid as well as dainty chalk hill blue butterflies. Watch for wheatears in summer; come the autumn, flocks of fieldfares and redwings can be seen stripping trees and bushes of their berries.

The view ahead suddenly opens out across the Oxford plain. Keep left at a fork and continue down to a gate in a fence. Once through this, bear right to pass beneath an old beech tree. The faint trail now drops steeply on to a sunken way. Turn left along this. It swings down to the left.

Don't go through the gate at the bottom; instead, turn sharp right Ⓑ. The M40 can't be ignored now as its passes through the Stokenchurch Gap just a few hundred yards away. Thankfully, the soft, grassy way soon swings away from the rush of the motorway, doubling back under Beacon Hill. Soon after the next gate, drop left to pass through two sets of gates in quick succession. Turn right along the track Ⓒ, following the route of the Icknield Way – also now the Ridgeway National Trail. Keep straight ahead and then cross the A40 to continue on the Ridgeway.

Almost ½ mile (750m) north-east of the A40, turn right at a crossing of bridleways Ⓓ. Ranks of deciduous trees dominate the undulating skyline ahead. A little way into the field, keep left to walk along what at first looks like an overgrown strip of land; a narrow trail, however, makes easy work of it. The bridleway then makes its way up into the woods. At a National

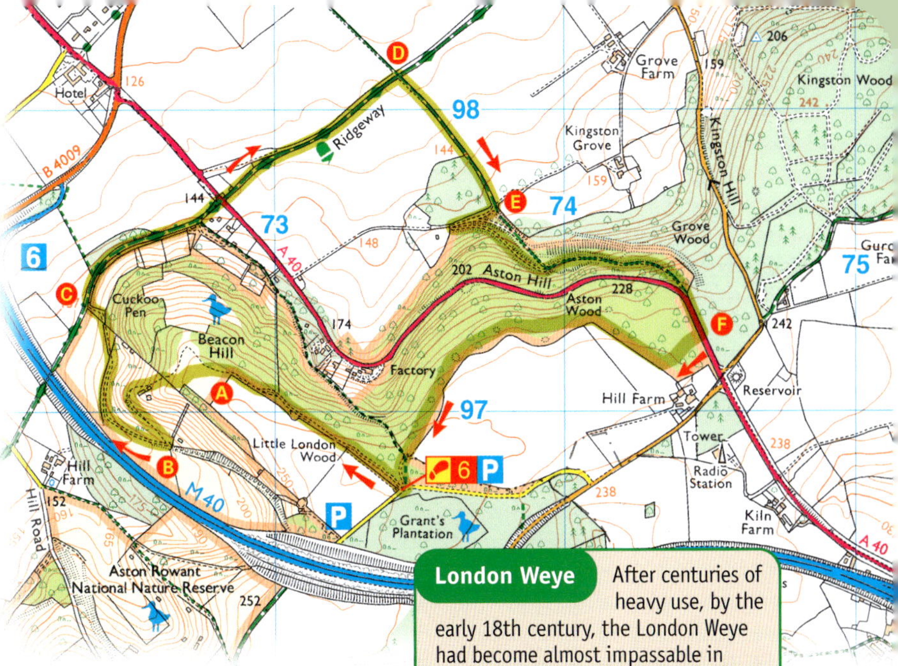

0 200 400 600 800 METRES 1 KILOMETRES
0 200 400 600 YARDS ½ MILES

SCALE 1:25 000 or 2½ INCHES to 1 MILE 4CM to 1KM

Trust sign on the edge of Juniper Bank **E**, take the trail on the right. On nearing a building, watch for a waymarker indicating a path doubling back sharply left. This is part of the medieval London Weye. Later rejoin the bridleway as it climbs from the left.

Turn left on reaching the A40. There's a trail on the grass verge to the left of the asphalt. Follow this for 150 yards or so and then cross to a layby to find a pedestrian gate **F** leading back into the woods. Beyond this, a trail heads left through the trees. It is marked at regular intervals by white arrows. Majestic old beech trees crown this ridge of high ground. In winter, once the leaves have fallen from the trees, distant views to the north-west come and go. This section of the route is particularly lovely on late spring evenings when the bluebells seem almost to glow as the sun lowers in the sky.

Bear right at a fork, still guided by white arrows. After a National Trust sign, ignore the path to the right. Keep straight on here, the white arrows quickly leading back to the parking area.

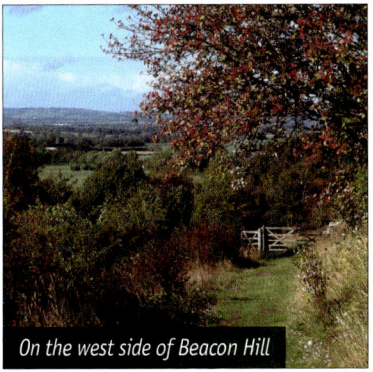

On the west side of Beacon Hill

London Weye After centuries of heavy use, by the early 18th century, the London Weye had become almost impassable in winter. To raise funds to maintain the medieval route linking Oxford with the capital, it became a turnpike, or toll road. Stagecoaches still struggled with the steep inclines though, and traffic was eventually diverted on to what is now the A40.

Stokenchurch Gap Blasted through the chalk escarpment in the early 1970s, this cutting features in the opening credits of the BBC comedy series *The Vicar of Dibley*.

walk 7

Stowe Park

Start
Chackmore, Buckinghamshire

Distance
4¼ miles (6.8km)

Height gain
290 feet (90m)

Approximate time
2 hours

Route terrain
Grassy paths, tracks and sealed lanes through estate parkland

Parking
Off-road parking at western edge of Chackmore, close to junction with Stowe Avenue

Dog friendly
This is a dog-friendly walk, but dogs should be on leads through parkland

OS maps
Landranger 152 (Northampton & Milton Keynes), Explorer 192 (Buckingham and Milton Keynes)

GPS waypoints
- SP 683 357
- Ⓐ SP 681 362
- Ⓑ SP 678 368
- Ⓒ SP 680 377
- Ⓓ SP 678 381
- Ⓔ SP 668 369

During the 18th century, Stowe Park was one of the finest landscaped gardens in southern England, but it was later left to decline. Today, the National Trust is slowly returning it to its former glory. By keeping to permissive paths and public rights of way, non-ticket holders can sample the delights of the parkland surrounding the gardens and see some of the many monuments and follies scattered across the site. The National Trust café, about ½ mile (800m) into the walk, is open to all.

> **Stowe** The landscaped gardens of Stowe were created by Viscount Cobham in the early 18th century. Over several decades, some of the country's top gardeners and architects, including Capability Brown, created lakes, planted trees and built monuments and temples here. By the time Stowe School gifted the grounds to the National Trust in 1989 though, many of these buildings were dilapidated and the gardens were a mess. Restoration work has already transformed the site and is likely to continue for many years.

Turn right along the road out of the parking area (away from Chackmore) and, immediately over the stream, take the trail on the right, keeping to the edge of the trees. This makes its way towards the grounds of Stowe Park, with the grand Corinthian Arch ahead. On reaching a surfaced lane Ⓐ, turn right and immediately left. The **café**, shop and other visitor facilities are soon on the right.

Reaching a fingerpost near a wooden hut Ⓑ, fork right - signposted 'Parkland' - and then quickly turn right again along a grassy path with a pink indicator at the start of it. Soon walk beside a low wall which, beyond two gates, becomes a fence. Turn left at a post with a yellow arrow on it, quickly crossing a bridge. After the gate, walk uphill beside the wall. After the next gate, keep straight ahead, along the field edge, now following public rights of way again. The building off to the right in the trees is the Bourbon Tower, first built in 1741 as the gamekeeper's house.

Nearing the far side of the field, turn left at a pink waymarker and immediately go right along the track Ⓒ. The Cobham Monument is on the left here. There are some impressive trees in this area, including several massive Spanish chestnuts and some unusual yellow-berried holly. Watch for flocks of long-tailed tits too.

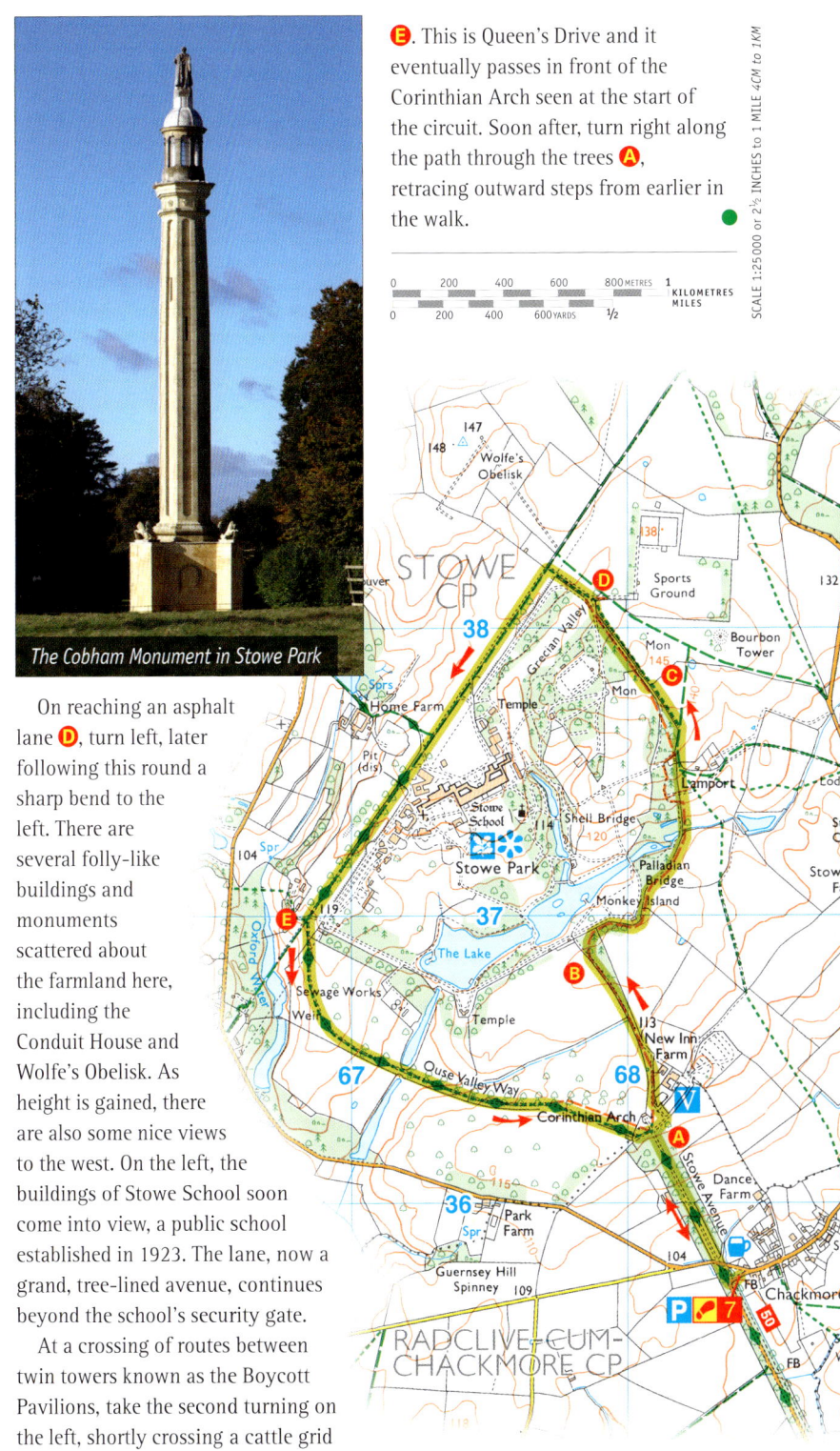

The Cobham Monument in Stowe Park

E. This is Queen's Drive and it eventually passes in front of the Corinthian Arch seen at the start of the circuit. Soon after, turn right along the path through the trees **A**, retracing outward steps from earlier in the walk. ●

On reaching an asphalt lane **D**, turn left, later following this round a sharp bend to the left. There are several folly-like buildings and monuments scattered about the farmland here, including the Conduit House and Wolfe's Obelisk. As height is gained, there are also some nice views to the west. On the left, the buildings of Stowe School soon come into view, a public school established in 1923. The lane, now a grand, tree-lined avenue, continues beyond the school's security gate.

At a crossing of routes between twin towers known as the Boycott Pavilions, take the second turning on the left, shortly crossing a cattle grid

STOWE PARK ● 25

walk 8

Walbury Hill

Start
Walbury Hill, Berkshire

Distance
4½ miles (7.4km)

Height gain
575 feet (175m)

Approximate time
2¼ hours

Route terrain
Good tracks; field paths, faint at first; quiet lanes; woodland

Parking
Combe Gibbet car park, 1½ miles (2.6km) south of Inkpen

Dog friendly
This is a dog-friendly walk

OS maps
Landranger 174 (Newbury & Wantage), Explorer 158 (Newbury and Hungerford)

GPS waypoints
SU 369 620
A SU 378 616
B SU 377 612
C SU 368 607
D SU 361 604
E SU 357 602
F SU 358 612
G SU 358 620

At 974 feet (297m) above sea level, Walbury Hill is the highest hill in south-east England. It is surrounded by the sleek, undulating lines of chalk country, giving rise to some excellent walking and some superb views. As well as visiting Walbury Hill and crossing Gallows Down, the scene of a grisly display in the 17th century, this short walk calls in at Combe, a delightful hamlet hidden in the folds of the hills.

Drop to the car park entrance and turn sharp left along the chalk track, keeping right when it forks. As height is gained on Walbury Hill, far-reaching views open to the north on a clear day. Sadly though, there is no public access to the trig pillar, so the route has to bypass the highest point. Just over ½ mile (1km) from the car park, turn right through a metal kissing-gate **A**. With no path on the ground to guide the way, drop south through the long grass to reach a pair of farm gates, from where there's a good view down to Combe. Don't go through the gates though; instead, continue in roughly the same direction, picking up a clearer trail as it makes its way through the bushes ahead and joins a bridleway.

After a small gate **B**, drop on to a byway, along which go right. This becomes a surfaced lane at Lower Farm. At a lane junction in Combe, turn left – towards Netherton. When the road performs a switchback to the left, continue straight ahead on a byway **C**. Up to the right in a few yards is St Swithun's Church, with its unusual part-timbered tower. The byway heads into the trees and begins ascending. The first part of the climb is rewarded by a great view of the surrounding downs, including Walbury Hill. The route then passes through a particularly atmospheric section of woodland, complete with ancient yews.

About 120 yards after crossing a track out in the open again, go through the wooden gate on the right **D**. The route of the bridleway is just discernable through the long grass as it heads west-south-west across Wadsmere Down. On entering the woods **E**, there are three path options. Take the middle one – just a narrow trail at first, but then bear left on joining a broader path. Keep right at a faint fork, along the clearer of the two routes. Emerging on a wide track, turn right, now following the route of the Test Way, a 43-mile (69-km) long-distance path from Walbury Hill to Southampton. Having walked the track for ¾ mile (1.2km), reach a dip **F**. The temptation here is to continue on the track, but turn right instead – through the gate.

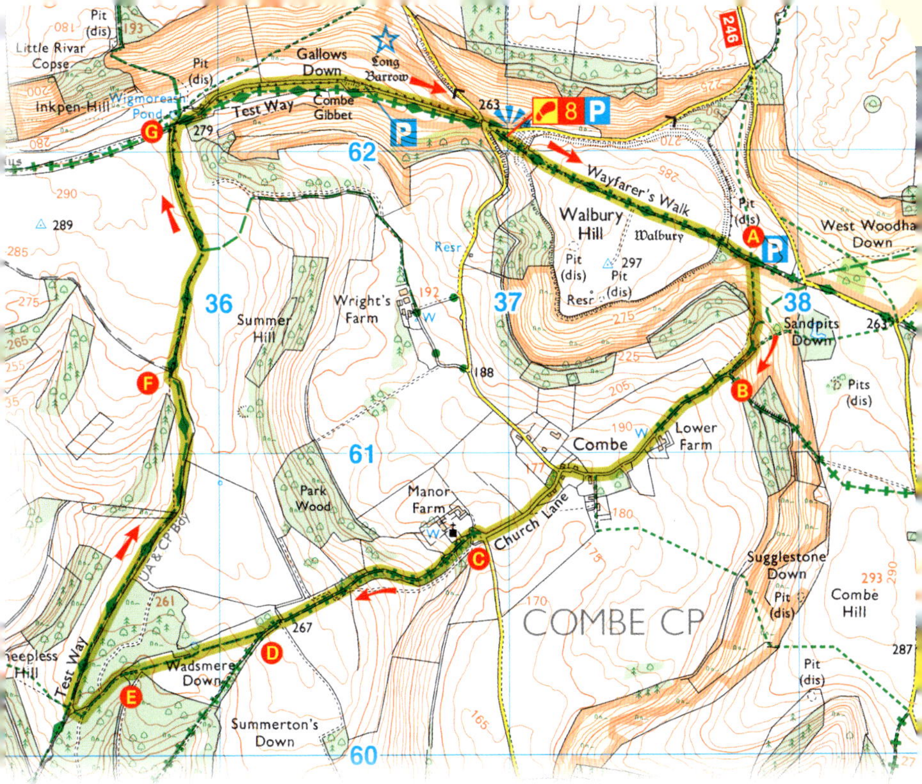

SCALE 1:25000 or 2½ INCHES to 1 MILE 4CM to 1KM

0 200 400 600 800 METRES 1 KILOMETRES
0 200 400 600 YARDS ½ MILES

Now head uphill beside the hedgerow on the right. When the hedgerow ends, the route swings slightly left of its previous line, continuing with another hedgerow to the left.

Turn right at a T-junction with a stony track **G**, soon gaining height again along the chalk ridge. This is Gallows Down, topped by Combe Gibbet to the left of the track. The track eventually drops to a road junction. Go straight across. The car park is on the right.

Combe Gibbet Gallows Down is the site of the 25-foot (7.6-m) high Combe Gibbet, a replica of the one used to display the bodies of George Broomham and Dorothy Newman after they were executed in Winchester in 1676. The pair had been having an adulterous affair and murdered Broomham's wife and son. Their corpses, suspended from one of the highest points in what was then Hampshire, would've been visible for miles around – a grisly warning to other would-be criminals.

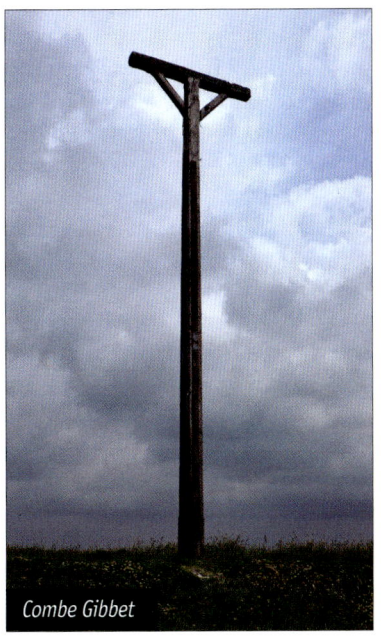

Combe Gibbet

walk 9

Brill

Start	Brill, Buckinghamshire
Distance	4¾ miles (7.7km)
Height gain	460 feet (140m)
Approximate time	2½ hours
Route terrain	Farmland; roads
Parking	Brill Windmill at top end of Windmill Street
Dog friendly	One awkward stile where dogs may need lifting between **B** and **C**
OS maps	Landranger 164 (Oxford), Explorer 180 (Oxford)
GPS waypoints	SP 652 141 **A** SP 645 141 **B** SP 635 133 **C** SP 625 141 **D** SP 631 151 **E** SP 639 151

From the moment you arrive in the parking area next to the 17th-century Brill Windmill, you just know you're in for a magical couple of hours. The views from this hilltop location are breathtaking. Be prepared too for your breath to be stolen at several other spots along this short but sweet walk. There's also an opportunity, on summer Sundays, to make a detour to the Boarstall Duck Decoy, once used to trap waterfowl and now managed by the National Trust.

From the car park entrance, turn right along the lane (South Hills) on the edge of Brill. About 70 yards after a track goes left, turn right along a trail through the vegetation. After a stile, keep to the left-hand side of the field for nearly 100 yards. Then go through the gap in the hedges and swing right, making for a stile about 40 yards left of the field corner. Having crossed this, continue in the same direction (west-north-west) down to a tiny bridge in a shallow dip. The path swings left here, through a kissing-gate and into a patch of woodland. Turn left at the road **A**.

Take the rough track to the left of the bend. This occupies a narrow strip of access land known as Span Green. When the stony track swings left, keep straight ahead along a grassier route. Keep straight on at all times, the ground underfoot later potentially muddy. Ignoring two waymarkers showing paths to the right, continue to the B4011, along which turn right. After walking on the road for about 150 yards, go through a small gate on the left **B**, just after the house.

Keep the field boundary on the left, watching for an easy-to-miss waymarker post on the left after just 120 yards. Turn right here, straight through the middle of the field (north-west), aiming for the right-hand edge of an area of woodland. Maintain the same line after a gate in a hedgerow. Go through a gate on the edge of the woodland and, almost immediately, turn left through another small gate to join a trail through the trees. After a stile, keep straight ahead, with the field boundary on the right. Enter another area of trees, negotiate a narrow plank bridge and then, in the next field,

> **Boarstall Duck Decoy** Duck decoys were invented in the 16th century to trap waterfowl. Birds, attracted by a fake duck placed on a small pond, would land nearby and be herded into netting tunnels from which they could not then escape. The example at Boarstall, one of only a few remaining in the UK, dates from the 1690s and is maintained today by the National Trust along with nearby Boarstall Tower, a 14th-century moated gatehouse.

head for the gate in the far right-hand corner **C**. (If in doubt, aim just to the right of the church at Boarstall.) Once through this, turn right along the quiet road through the village, later passing the signposted track up to the Duck Decoy on the left. (To visit, it's just over ½ mile/1km there and back.)

Turn left at the T-junction with the B4011. Having walked the asphalt for 450 yards, reach the Oxfordshire county border sign. Immediately after this, turn right through a gate **D** and walk uphill with a hedgerow on the left. Go through the gate in the top corner and keep right, walking with a fence/hedgerow on the right. On the climb, take some time to look behind at the ever-improving outlook to the west. Keep close to the field boundary all the while and eventually reach a road **E**. Turn right along this.

It's now slightly more than ½ mile (1km) of road walking back to Brill, but the lane is quiet and enjoys tremendous views. Soon after a crossroads, head uphill, passing the Brill village sign. Later, drawing level with a track on the left, meet two trails on the right. Take the left-hand option, making almost directly for the windmill. It emerges on the flat area to the left of the building (open summer Sunday afternoons). The parking area is on the left. ●

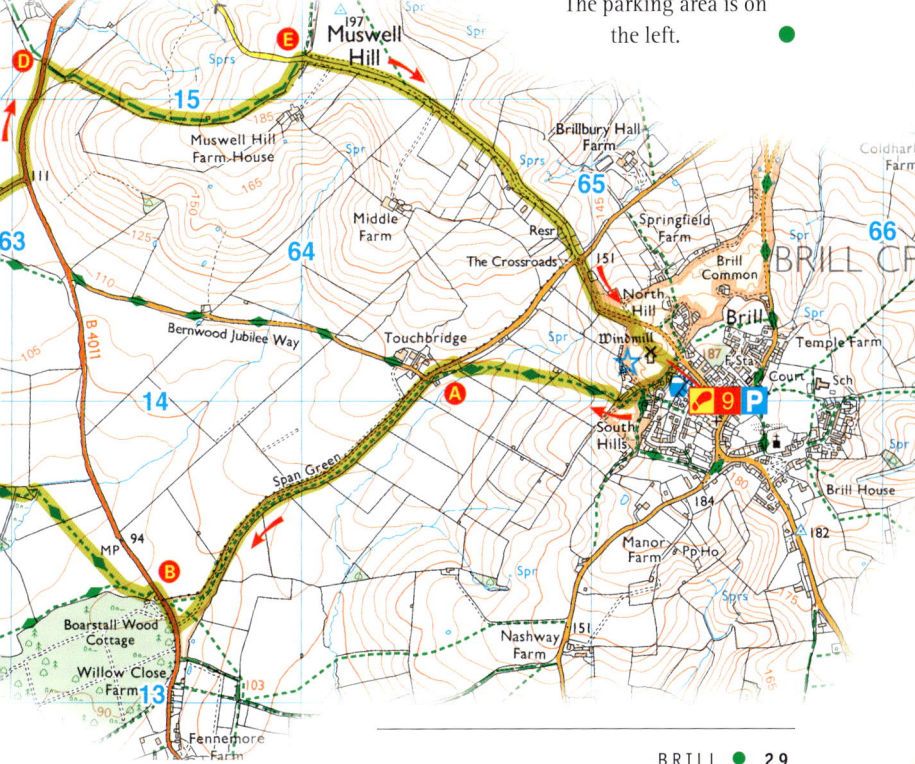

SCALE 1:25000 or 2½ INCHES to 1 MILE 4CM to 1KM

BRILL ● 29

walk 10

Greenham Common and the Kennet & Avon Canal

Start
Greenham Common, Berkshire

Distance
5 miles (8.1km)

Height gain
200 feet (60m)

Approximate time
2½ hours

Route terrain
Surfaced trails through reserve; rough tracks; canal towpath

Parking
Greenham Common Control Tower car park, signposted off Bury's Bank Road, 1 mile (1.6km) east of Greenham

Dog friendly
Yes, but on leads on reserve during nesting season

OS maps
Landranger 174 (Newbury & Wantage), Explorer 158 (Newbury & Hungerford)

GPS waypoints

- SU 499 651
- Ⓐ SU 510 647
- Ⓑ SU 516 651
- Ⓒ SU 521 661
- Ⓓ SU 497 667
- Ⓔ SU 501 654

This really is a walk of two halves. It first visits Greenham Common where the spectre of the former US Air Force base's Cold War history survives alongside a wide variety of birds, plants and mammals on Berkshire's largest area of open heath. The second half takes in a tranquil stretch of the Kennet & Avon Canal, passing locks and the wildlife-rich Thatcham Reedbeds along the way.

 Take the path to the right of the control tower (home to a **café**). Soon after the gate, turn left at a T-junction. Go straight over two path crossings. The path then bends left as another joins from the right. Visitors are immediately struck by the size of this flat, open area of heathland, once the site of the longest military runway in Europe, built to cope with some of the US Air Force's largest planes. After a long, straight stretch of path, take the first turning on the left Ⓐ. Winding round the edge of the reserve, follow this path for over ½ mile (almost 1km) and then go through a gate on the left. Cross the road and take the track opposite Ⓑ.

The track leads beneath trees to a junction. Turn left along a surfaced lane. After crossing the River Kennet keep straight ahead – picking up another rough track beyond Chamberhouse

Greenham peace camp

Greenham Common was a Royal Air Force and, later, a US Air Force base that, during the early decades of the Cold War, was used by massive US planes capable of carrying nuclear bombs. In 1980 though, it was announced that ground-launched cruise missiles would be sited here, part of the West's nuclear deterrent against the USSR. A women's peace camp was set up to protest against this. Over the next 19 years, tens of thousands of women joined the encampment, attracting global media attention. One of the most famous moments in the protest's long story came in 1982 when 30,000 women joined hands around the base's perimeter fence. Although the last cruise missile left Greenham Common in 1991, small numbers of protesters stayed until 2000 – partly to ensure public access and commoners' rights were reinstated. They were, and much of the former airbase is today managed by the Berkshire, Buckinghamshire and Oxfordshire Wildlife Trust.

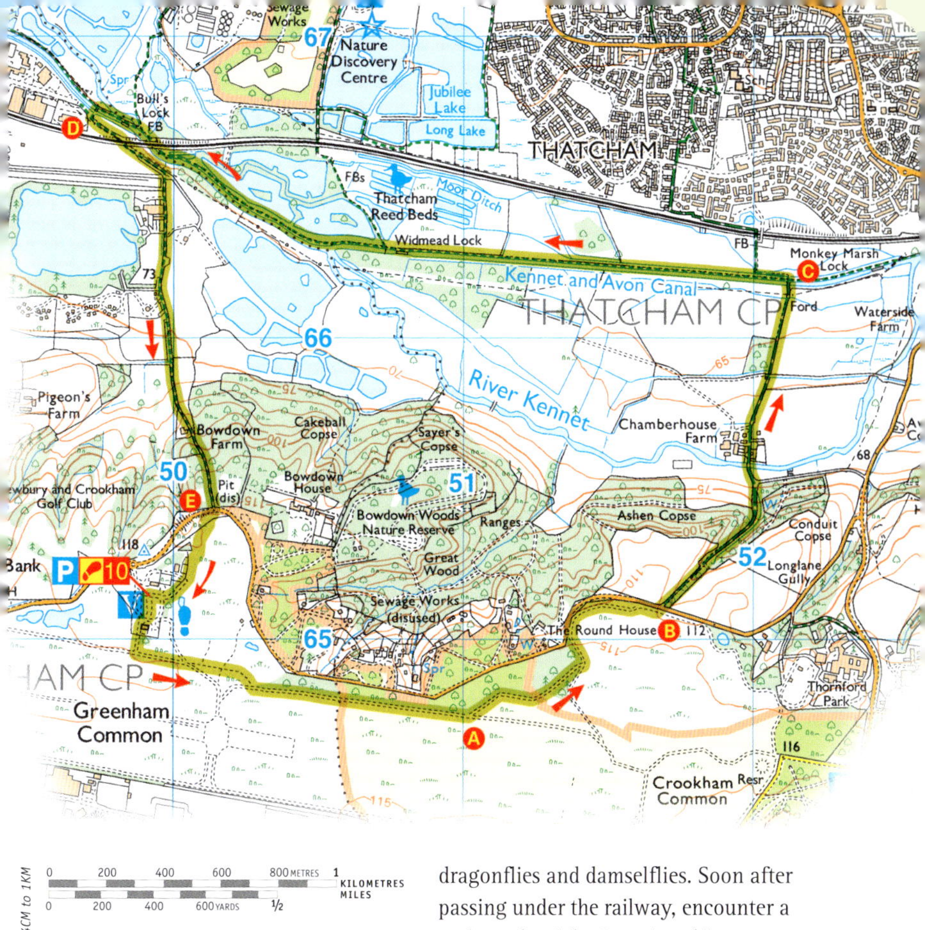

Farm. Cross the bridge over the Kennet and Avon Canal **C**. Turn left and walk along the towpath for 1½ miles (2.5km). Along the way, pass Widmead Lock and the Thatcham Reedbeds, home to warblers, terns and at least 14 species of dragonflies and damselflies. Soon after passing under the railway, encounter a path on the right. Ignoring this, continue on the towpath for now. Then, about 130 yards beyond Bull's Lock, turn left to cross the bridge over the canal. Go left again, along the road **D**. When this splits after passing back under the railway, take the right-hand option. At the gates at the far end of Newbury Racecourse, turn sharp right. When this narrow lane ends, keep straight ahead through a gate, joining a track from the left. This eventually comes out at Bury's Bank Road **E**.

Cross diagonally left and follow the faint trail up through the trees. Re-entering the Greenham Common reserve, go through the gate and turn right. Go right at the next junction and right again after a gate. After one more gate, turn left and return to the control tower.

Greenham Common's control tower

GREENHAM COMMON AND THE KENNET & AVON CANAL

walk 11

Hurley, Ashley Hill and the River Thames

Start
Hurley, Berkshire

Distance
5¼ miles (8.5km)

Height gain
425 feet (130m)

Approximate time
2½ hours

Route terrain
Quiet lanes; farmland; woodland; riverside

Parking
Village car park in Hurley

Dog friendly
This is a dog-friendly walk

OS maps
Landranger 175 (Reading & Windsor), Explorer 172 (Chiltern Hills East)

GPS waypoints
- SU 825 840
- Ⓐ SU 827 831
- Ⓑ SU 824 811
- Ⓒ SU 812 822
- Ⓓ SU 810 834
- Ⓔ SU 825 841

With two pubs and lots of attractive, historic buildings, the riverside village of Hurley is a lovely place to start a walk. The route starts by heading away from the River Thames and climbing to Ashley Hill where the mixed woodland provides pleasant walking, particularly when the tall, elegant conifers are swaying in the breeze. Passing a small nature reserve on the way, you then reach the river at Frogmill, from where a gorgeous stretch of the Thames Path leads back to Hurley.

Walk back out of Hurley along the lane just driven to reach the car park. (There is pavement all the way.) Pass the village shop and two pubs on the way – **The Olde Bell** and the **Rising Sun**. At the A4130, turn right and immediately cross the road to take the path through the metal gate opposit Ⓐ. After a stiff but short climb up Prospect Hill, keep straight ahead through High Wood. Emerging from the trees, maintain the same line – beside fields. At a surfaced lane, cross diagonally right and head through the middle of a field. Beyond a small patch of woodland and another field path, cross a quiet lane. Enter the woods and keep right at an early fork. After a climb, step up on to a broad track, part of the Berkshire Loop of the Chiltern Way. Turn right here.

Rise to the gates of a house occupying the highest point on Ashley Hill Ⓑ, go right again. Reaching a broad track, cross over to continue on a narrower path. Emerging on a track, continue in the same direction. After passing a house, take the second footpath on the left. (The two path turnings are close together.) Turn right along a surfaced track. Just before this ends at a metal gate, swing off on the bridleway, keeping close to the fence on the left. This later drops on to another bridleway joining from the left Ⓒ.

At the A4130, turn left and then take the lane to Frogmill on the right. Past some buildings, this swings right. As it does so, go left Ⓓ to reach the river. Turn right along the Thames Path and keep the river to the left for the next 1¼ miles (1.9km). Nearing Hurley though, don't be tempted to keep to the track that swings away from the water's edge. Instead, stay on the riverbank, soon crossing a bridge. Nearing a footbridge over the

> **Hurley Priory** The Benedictine priory of St Mary's was established as a cell of Westminster Abbey in 1086. Parts of the Norman structure survive today – in the parish church and in a neighbouring private house. The hostelry run by the monks is now The Olde Bell inn which, after nearly 900 years of welcoming guests, claims to be the oldest hotel in the UK.

The priory church of St Mary's at Hurley

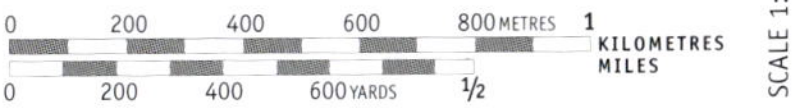

navigable channel, take the path on the right and then go right again along a surfaced path **E**. Just after the gate into Tithecote Manor, turn right to re-enter the car park where the walk began.

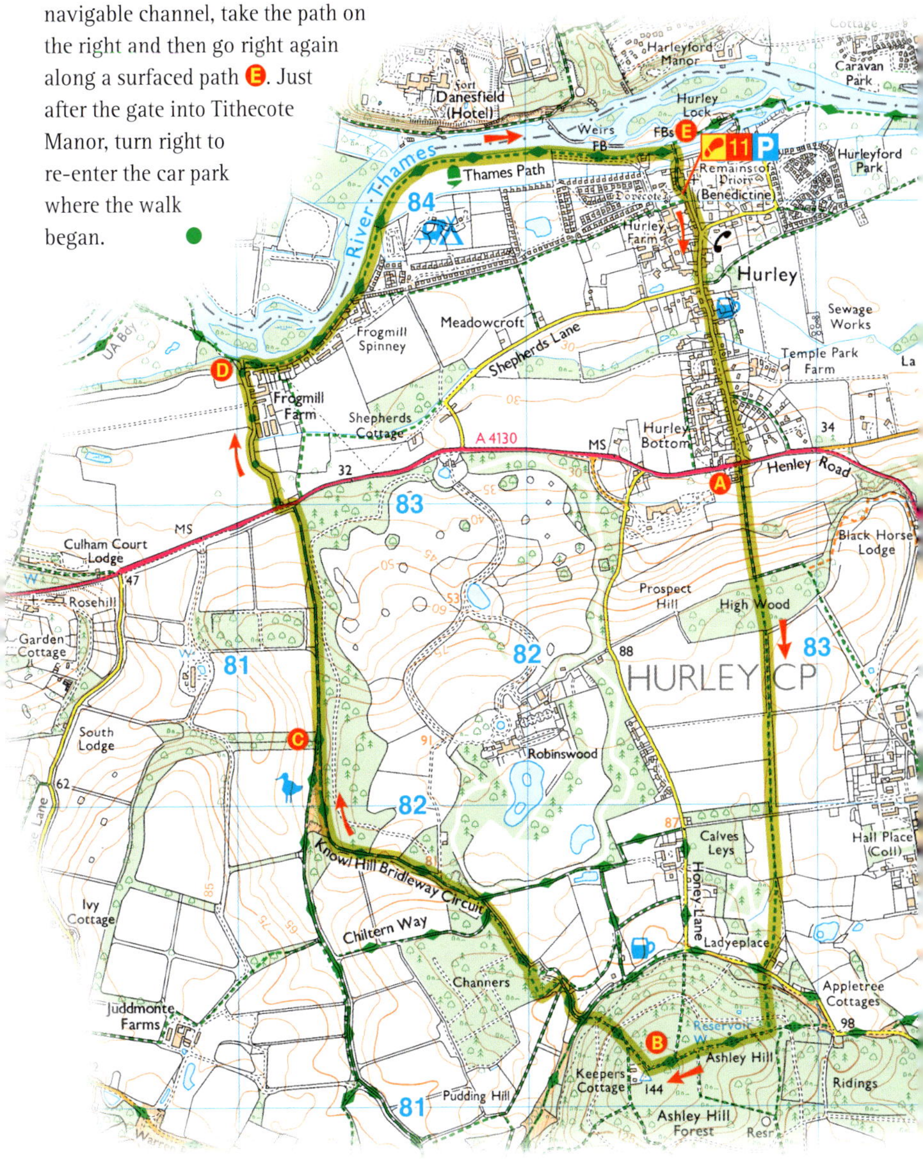

HURLEY, ASHLEY HILL AND THE RIVER THAMES • 33

walk 12

River Thames at Shiplake

Start
Shiplake Station, Oxfordshire

Distance
5½ miles (9km)

Height gain
170 feet (50m)

Approximate time
2½ hours

Route terrain
Riverside; good tracks; woodland; quiet lanes

Parking
There is limited roadside parking in Shiplake; it is better to arrive by train. Those with time might want to consider walking the Thames Path from Henley (2 miles/ 3.2km), where parking is more plentiful, and joining the route at **F**

Dog friendly
Yes, but dogs on leads through private gardens

OS maps
Landranger 175 (Reading & Windsor), Explorer 171 (Chiltern Hills West)

GPS waypoints
- SU 776 797
- **A** SU 780 795
- **B** SU 777 787
- **C** SU 768 781
- **D** SU 758 785
- **E** SU 761 798
- **F** SU 775 804

What better way to start a walk than with a riverside stroll? And not just any river, but the beautiful River Thames. Having got off the train at Shiplake, walkers head down to the Thames Path and follow England's most famous river upstream. The delights continue even when you head away from the water's edge, with the route continuing through attractive woodland and along quiet tracks and lanes that provide a glimpse of some of the luxurious properties that grace this part of Oxfordshire.

Having left the platform at Shiplake Station, turn left along the road and then, after **The Baskerville** pub, go left again. After 400 yards, take the path on the left. This is part of the Thames Path, a National Trail that follows the river from its source in the Cotswolds to the Thames Barrier near Greenwich. It winds its way through the trees and under the railway. Duck your head! Aim for the gate on the other side of the open area, but don't go through it. Instead, turn right, walking with a

Messing about on the water

34 ● WALK 12

fence on the left. Follow this round to the left, over a bridge, and then continue to the river. After a gate **A** step onto the path beside the Thames. The route goes right here (upstream), but first have a look at the information panel to the left to find out more about

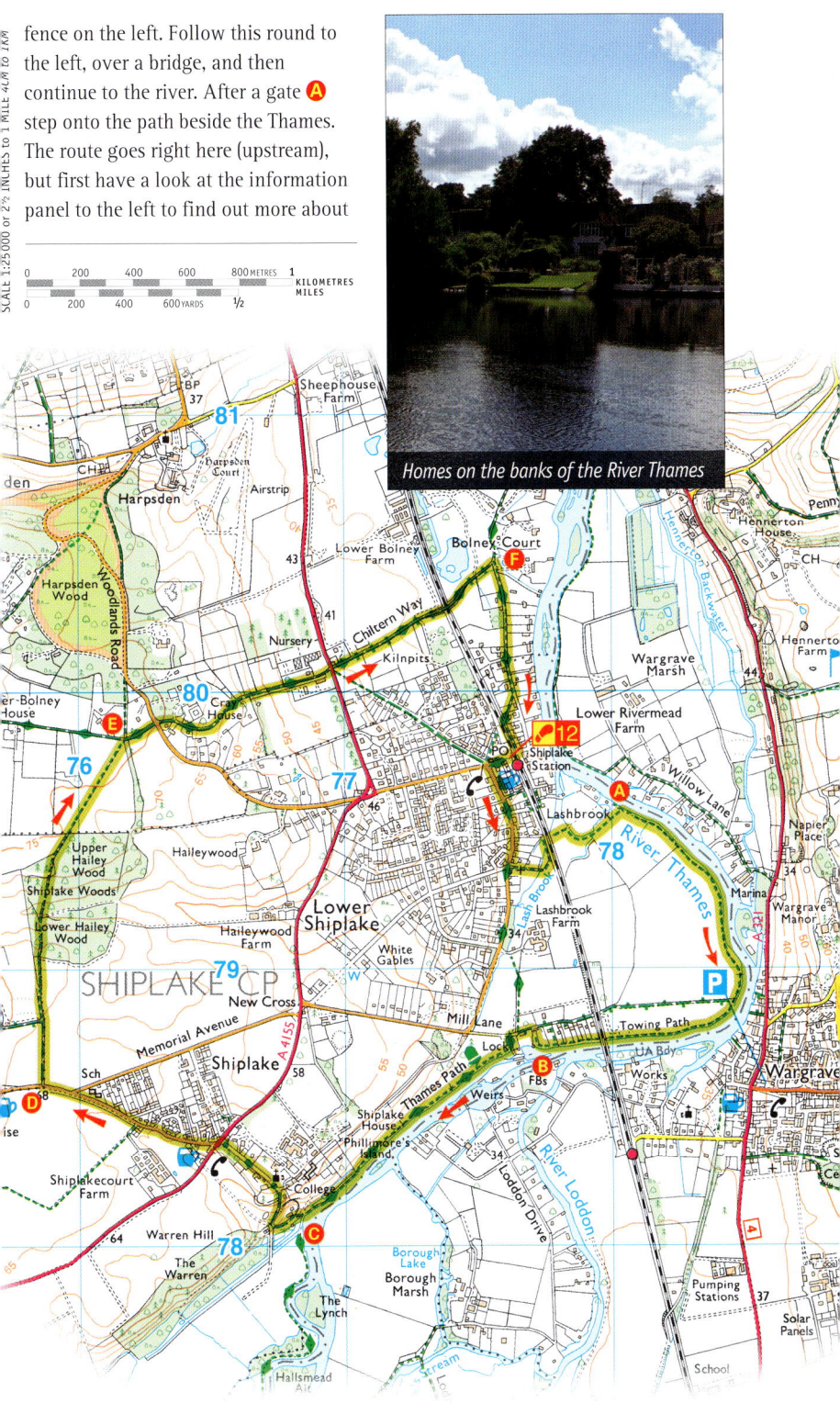

Homes on the banks of the River Thames

RIVER THAMES AT SHIPLAKE • 35

> **George Orwell** The writer, born Eric Blair in 1903, moved to Shiplake with his family when he was a child after his father retired from the Indian civil service. Probably best known for his novels *Animal Farm* and *1984*, he used to fish on the River Thames near his home. His love of the activity formed an important part of his 1939 book, *Coming up for Air*, in which narrator George Bowling escapes suburban life by revisiting the countryside where he fished as a boy.

the Lashbrook Ferry, which operated from a nearby house from the 1770s until 1953.

The next 1¾ miles (2.9km) of almost uninterrupted riverside walking are an absolute delight. There are some gorgeous properties on the far bank and boats come and go all the time. After passing under the railway, go through a tall gate to begin an unusual stretch of walking – across several private gardens that lead all the way down to the riverbank. *Please make sure you close each of the garden gates and keep dogs on leads.* After about 200 yards of this, watch carefully for an easy-to-miss sign on a gate indicating that the path performs a kink ⓑ. In this garden, turn right, pass to the left of the house and out through a gate. Go left along the lane and, in just 100 yards, take the surfaced path on the left to regain the riverside route near Shiplake Lock.

At a Shiplake College sign, swing away from the Thames and pass to the immediate right of the waterside clubhouse ⓒ. There a gravel track heads through the trees and bushes ahead. Follow this to a surfaced lane. Turn right, along a path just before the lane. Emerging at Shiplake church, join the lane heading left. On reaching the A4155, cross diagonally left to join Plough Lane. The pavement runs out on passing the turning for Memorial Avenue. Continue for a further 120 yards and then take the surfaced lane on the right ⓓ. When this bends left, keep straight ahead – along a path between trees and hedgerows. Continue in the same direction through tranquil Shiplake Woods. On the far side of a field, turn right along a surfaced lane ⓔ. Go straight across a road to continue on a gravel track, now following part of the southern extension to the 134-mile (215-km) Chiltern Way. The route goes straight over the A4155 as well and soon passes the grounds of the Black Bears Polo Club.

Reaching a T-junction ⓕ, turn right. Follow this lane for 500 yards and then turn right along the signposted Thames Path. This quickly crosses a track to pass between high hedges. At the railway, don't cross the stile; instead, turn left. Keep forward to a lane and turn right. Once over the level crossing, the station is over to the left.

Cruisers on the River Thames at Shiplake

Slightly harder walks of 3–3½ hours

The gently undulating landscape of the Chilterns

walk 13

Milton-under-Wychwood and Bruern Abbey

Start	Milton-under-Wychwood, Oxfordshire
Distance	6 miles (9.7km)
Height gain	320 feet (100m)
Approximate time	3 hours
Route terrain	Country lanes; tracks; woodland; field paths; short section through village
Parking	Village green car park in Milton-under-Wychwood
Dog friendly	This is a dog-friendly walk
OS maps	Landranger 163 (Cheltenham & Cirencester), Explorer OL45 (The Cotswolds)
GPS waypoints	SP 264 183
Ⓐ	SP 270 193
Ⓑ	SP 263 203
Ⓒ	SP 257 210
Ⓓ	SP 253 205
Ⓔ	SP 240 188
Ⓕ	SP 253 186

Honey-coloured Cotswold settlements, pretty woods, gently rolling farmland and an 18th-century country house are some of the features on this relatively short walk from the village of Milton-under-Wychwood in the Evenlode valley. Among the springtime highlights are the bluebells of the Berkshire, Buckinghamshire and Oxfordshire Wildlife Trust's Foxholes Nature Reserve. The route also calls in at the attractive village of Fifield.

 From the gate leading into the car park, walk straight across the grassy area, passing between a tennis court (left) and a children's adventure play area. On the far side, go through a kissing-gate and turn left, walking with a fence on the right. Emerging on a track, go left, passing a cottage on the right. The shady path, ending at a stile, comes out on the Lyneham Road, along which turn right.

Having followed this quiet lane for nearly ½ mile (750m), turn left along the signposted bridleway Ⓐ, following the route of the Oxfordshire Way. When the fence on the right ends, keep straight on, along the field edge, enjoying views across the Evenlode valley. Beyond a few trees, continue along a broad ride through the woodland, with Bruern Abbey directly ahead. After a gate, continue in the same direction, through the middle of the field. Beyond the next gate, the bridleway keeps straight ahead, soon passing to the left of Bruern Abbey's gardens. Reaching some railings, bear left – away from the railings.

A gate leads on to a road Ⓑ. Cross this to continue on the signposted Oxfordshire Way. Soon walk in the company of a fence on the right and Cocksmoor Copse on the left. The path, muddy at times, then passes through some woodland. About 100 yards after brushing up against the River Evenlode, a

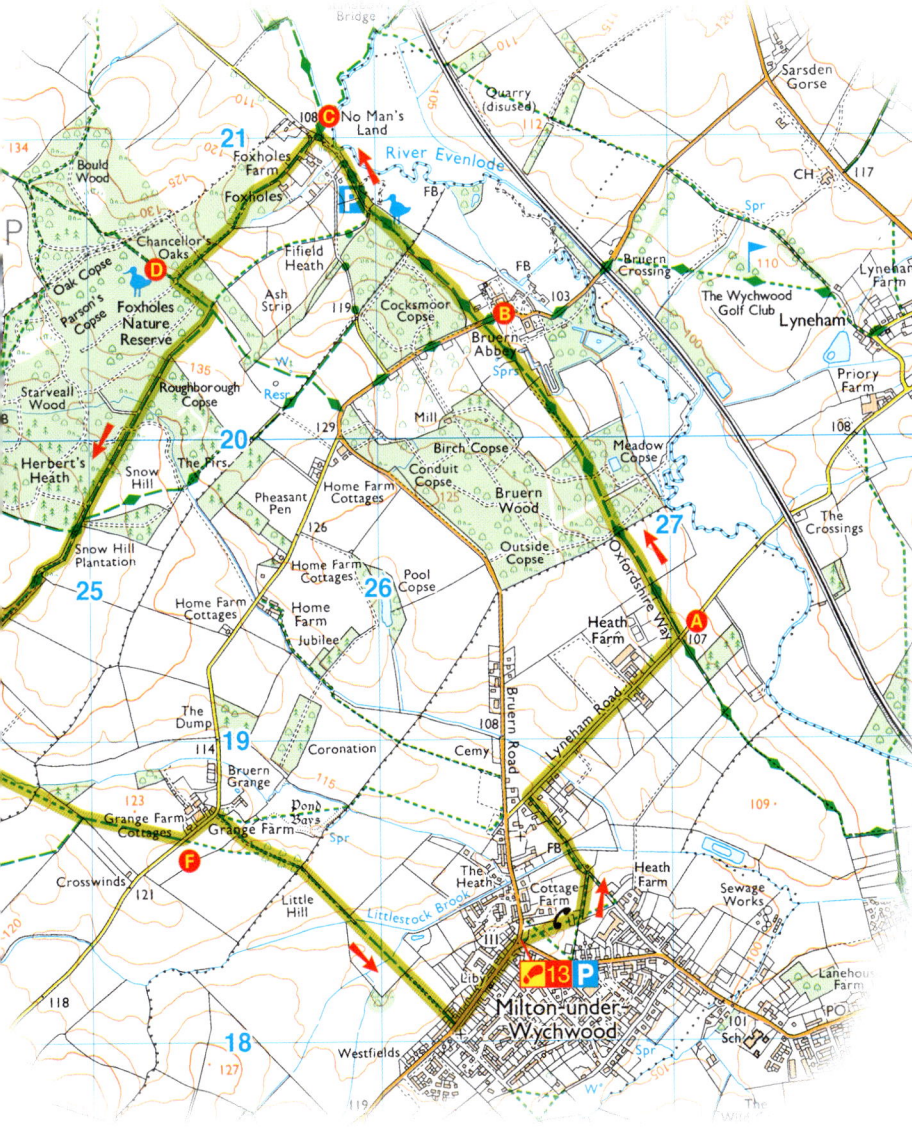

T-junction is reached. The path to the right heads out of the woods, but our

> **Bruern Abbey** The house, with its imposing Georgian façade, was built in about 1720 close to the site of a Cistercian abbey established in 1147. It briefly housed a private school in the second half of the 20th century but has now returned to private ownership.

route goes left. Keep left when stepping up on to a broad track ⓒ. At the gate to Foxholes House, bear right and then immediately left, keeping close to the property's boundary fence. Go through a large wooden gate and follow the track into the woods. At a path junction near the edge of the Foxholes Nature

SCALE 1:25000 or 2½ INCHES to 1 MILE 4CM to 1KM

MILTON-UNDER-WYCHWOOD AND BRUERN ABBEY • 39

The stone-built cottages of Fifield

Reserve, turn right, keeping to the bridleway along the forest edge for now. The woods here are gorgeous at any time of the year but are particularly charming in spring when they are carpeted with bluebells.

Heading deeper into the trees, arrive at a path junction near a bench **D**. Go left here. Stepping out into the open again, turn right, keeping close to the trees on the right. Following an almost dead-straight line, the bridleway heads back into the trees. It can be wet in places, but trails have developed to bypass the marshiest ground. Keep straight ahead on joining a track from the left. When this quickly swings right, maintain the previous direction, now on a grassy path. This tree-lined path, overgrown in places, winds its way across the farmland. Bear left at a fork. After a gate, bear left on joining a more obvious path.

Coming to Fifield, turn left along the road **E** and then almost immediately left again along a rough lane between some cottages. At the lane-end, go through a small gate beside a larger one on the left. Walk downhill to find a small gate tucked away in the bottom right-hand corner of this recreational area. Go through this and follow a line of power poles east across the field. After a gap in the hedges, maintain this heading across a second field, aiming for a large gate, but coming away from the power lines. Beyond this gate, continue in the same direction, ignoring the tempting track up to the left. Soon walk with a stream on the left. Go through a kissing-gate in the hedges, cross a bridge and bear left to walk along the field edge, soon heading uphill. In the field corner, go through the gates on the left and head diagonally across the field, aiming slightly right of Grange Farm Cottages ahead.

A pair of gates leads on to a narrow road **F**, along which turn left. Drawing level with some buildings on the left, turn right through a gate. The bridleway follows a track which soon passes through another gate and then continues between the fields. When the track ends, go through the gate and continue on the same line. Cross a small brook, go through a gate and follow a line of power poles towards Milton-under-Wychwood. A gravel track leads to the road; turn left here. Just after passing **The Hare** pub on the right, look for the entrance to the parking area on the left as the road bends right.

Pishill and Stonor Park

Start
Pishill, Oxfordshire

Distance
6 miles (9.7km)

Height gain
795 feet (240m)

Approximate time
3 hours

Route terrain
Woodland; field paths; deer park; short sections on roads

Parking
Car park beside Pishill church (honesty box in porch)

Dog friendly
One awkward stile where dogs may need lifting at **E**

OS maps
Landranger 175 (Reading & Windsor), Explorer 171 (Chiltern Hills West)

GPS waypoints
- SU 726 898
- **A** SU 723 887
- **B** SU 723 883
- **C** SU 736 889
- **D** SU 747 892
- **E** SU 753 898
- **F** SU 751 902
- **G** SU 743 909
- **H** SU 732 902

Starting from the tiny hamlet of Pishill, you'll enjoy ever-changing views on this undulating walk in the Chilterns. The route winds its way in and out of woodland and across farmland as it makes for the village of Stonor. From here, it enters Stonor Park, with glimpses of Stonor House and, if you're lucky, the fallow deer that inhabit the parkland. The gorgeous Oxfordshire countryside slowly reveals itself as the route dips and climbs and dips again on its return to Pishill.

Leave the car park and turn right along the lane. About 100 yards beyond the Old Vicarage's driveway, bear left along a rough track. The bridleway splits here. Head left, out into the open and downhill along the field edge. At a track on the edge of Pishillbury Wood, go straight across, soon climbing steeply through the trees. Nearing some houses at Maidensgrove, bear left at a fork marked by white arrows on the trees. Take the narrower of the two routes on the far side of the next road **A**. Again, the route is indicated by a white arrow. Leaving the trees, continue in the same direction and, on the far side of this open area, bear left along the field edge. Just before reaching the hedgerow at Lodge Farm, turn sharp left **B** – back across the field, heading east-north-east.

White arrows guide the way through Park Wood. Beyond the trees, keep straight ahead, passing through two fields and two gates before reaching the road at Stonor village. Turn left and

The route passes through Stonor House's rolling parkland, home to fallow deer

walk along the asphalt for about 350 yards. On the village edge, there are some high metal railings on the right. At the 'private deer park' sign, go through the gate in them **C**. Gradually moving away from the fence on the right and aiming to the right of a small group of trees, head straight up the slope in front (east), following signs for Southend and the Chiltern Way. There's no path on the ground at first, but it soon becomes clearer and there are arrows on the trees to use as a guide. Height is quickly gained, and grand views open out across the delightful parkland to Stonor House. The path crosses two tracks. Watch for a sign pointing down to **Chilterns' Pit Stop Café** (limited opening hours) on the way across the deer park.

Enter the woods via a deer gate **D**. The narrow trail soon joins a wider path from the left. Turn left on reaching a lane near Southend and then take the surfaced track on the right. After 100 yards, cross the stile **E** set back in the vegetation on the left. Walk with the hedgerow on the left and then cross a lane diagonally left to continue along the field edge. After two gates in quick succession, cut across the field corner to enter Summerheath Wood **F**. (Look to the right just before the woods for a lovely view of the countryside around Turville.)

There are lots of trails in these woods. Simply continue in the same direction as before (north-west) until coming to a lane. Turn left along this and keep right when the road quickly forks. Keep straight on as another lane goes left and go on to reach a road junction. Cross and take the gravel track opposite. The route continues by taking a footpath to the left of the gate into Saviours **G**. Stay close to the hedge on the left at first and a faint trail materialises,

> **Stonor House** This grand house has been the Stonor family's home for more than 850 years, with some parts of it dating from the 12th century. In the 16th century, the family provided refuge for the Jesuit priest Edmund Campion. A press was smuggled into the house and assembled in the roof space to enable him to print a pamphlet illegally outlining why Catholicism was preferable to the post-Reformation Church of England. He was hung, drawn and quartered for treason in 1581 and then canonised as a martyr in 1970.

heading south-west across open pasture. After three more gates, turn right along an enclosed track. Reaching a high point on the track, the views to the south open out. A handy bench provides a great place to sit and soak up the

surroundings. The path now dips, crosses a track **H** and then climbs again. At a pair of locked gates, head to the left of the tree beside them to access a lane. Go straight across and follow an overgrown path downhill beside a fence. Reaching a wider path, turn left. Go right at the road and then take the lane on the left. The car park is to the right in 150 yards.

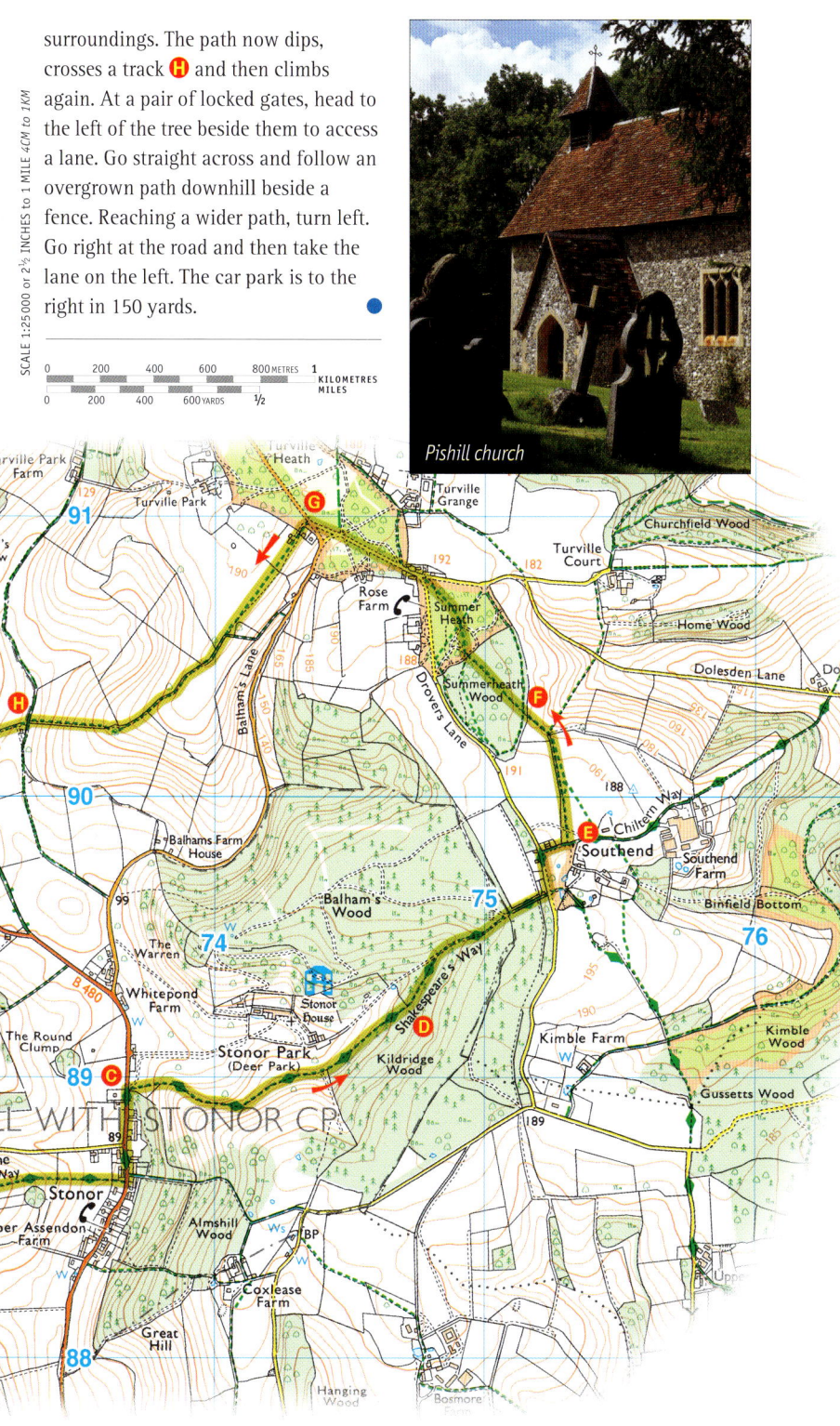

Pishill church

PISHILL AND STONOR PARK • 43

walk 15

Windsor Great Park and Virginia Water

Start
Virginia Water, Berkshire

Distance
6 miles (9.8km)

Height gain
360 feet (110m)

Approximate time
3 hours

Route terrain
Mostly surfaced paths through parkland

Parking
Virginia Water South car park (height barrier)

Dog friendly
This is a dog-friendly walk

OS maps
Landranger 175 (Reading & Windsor), Explorer 160 (Windsor, Weybridge & Bracknell)

GPS waypoints

- SU 960 687
- Ⓐ SU 961 689
- Ⓑ SU 979 697
- Ⓒ SU 978 703
- Ⓓ SU 972 710
- Ⓔ SU 974 714
- Ⓕ SU 971 711
- Ⓖ SU 968 699
- Ⓗ SU 959 690

A former royal hunting ground, Windsor Great Park covers almost 5,000 acres (2,000 hectares) to the south of Windsor Castle, taking in woodland, immense lawns, gardens and lakes. This walk explores just a tiny fraction of the area, starting with a visit to Virginia Water, an artificial lake created in the mid-18th century. Surprisingly tranquil beyond the popular lakeside path, it's a very varied walk with lots of interesting features along the way. Large numbers of ring-necked parakeets, increasingly common in parts of south-east England, add an exotic touch.

Locate the wooden pay station on the north side of the car park, go through the gate on its far side and then keep straight ahead on a path through the trees. On reaching the surfaced path beside Virginia Water, turn right Ⓐ. This is now followed for 1¾ miles (almost 3km), past the Roman Ruins, the Cascade and then, after briefly coming away from the water's edge, the **Pavilion Café** at the entrance to the main Virginia Water car park. (The county border with Surrey is crossed along the way.)

The path swings left to cross the Wick Pond Causeway. Keep to the surfaced route, soon passing to the right of the Totem Pole and then climbing between high laurel hedges. As the track then swings left, take the path to the right Ⓑ. This is not the route going right at a 90-degree angle, but the one continuing straight ahead between the hedges.

Go straight across a broad, surfaced track. About 100 yards short of The Savill Garden car park, turn sharp left Ⓒ – almost doubling back. Very soon reach a surfaced path beside the Obelisk Pond. Turn right along this. Take the next path on the

> **Windsor Great Park** The first castle at Windsor was established by William the Conqueror, who used the surrounding grassland and woods as a hunting ground. Many of the features visitors see today though were added from the 18th century onwards. Work on creating the lake at Virginia Water, for example, began in 1752. The Ruins contain stonework from the Roman city of Leptis Magna in modern-day Libya, brought to England in the early 19th century. The Totem Pole, meanwhile, was a gift to Queen Elizabeth II from the Canadians in the 1950s.

0 200 400 600 800 METRES 1 KILOMETRES
0 200 400 600 YARDS ½ MILES

SCALE 1:25 000 or 2½ INCHES to 1 MILE *4CM to 1KM*

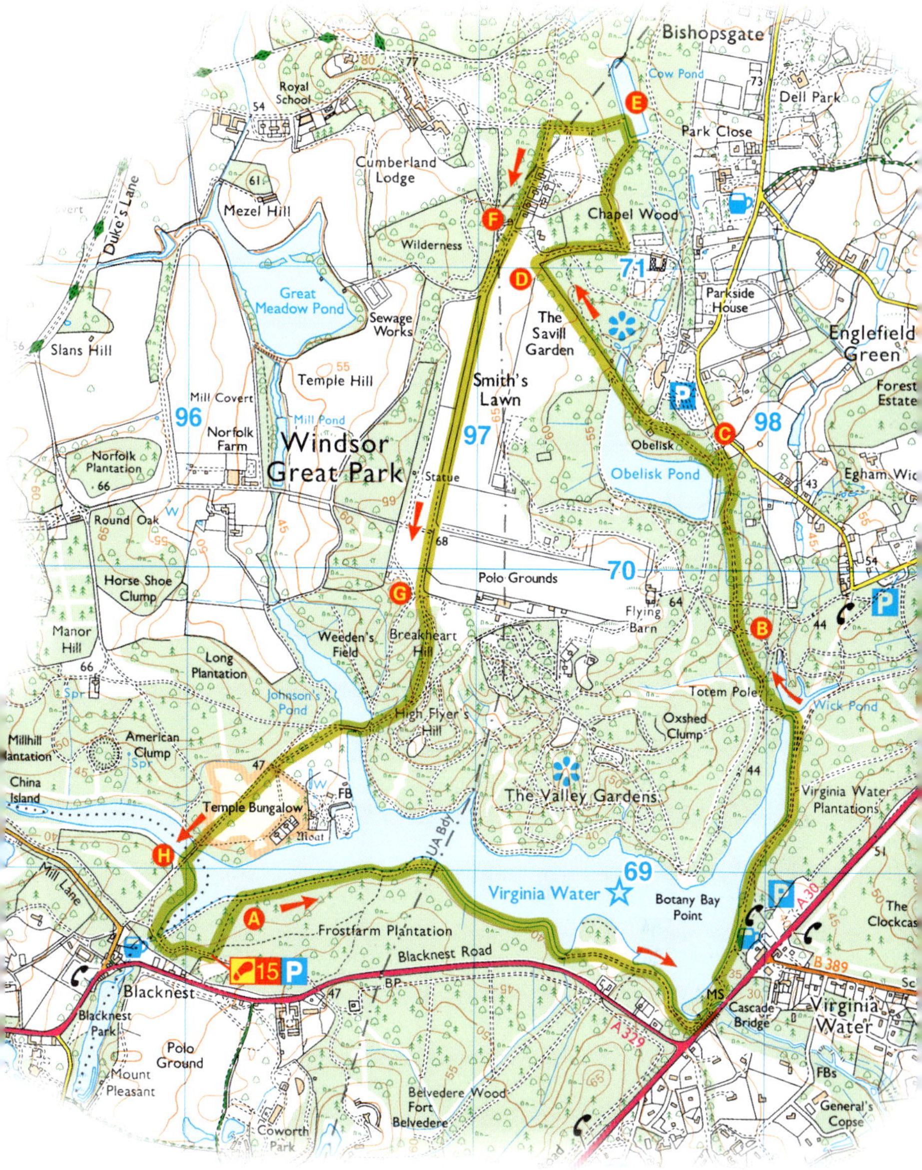

left, passing close to the Cumberland Obelisk, erected by George II in honour of his son, the Duke of Cumberland, known for his brutal suppression of the Jacobite Rebellion of 1745.

After crossing the bridge, ignore the path to the left and simply keep straight ahead on a trail beside the fence and hedgerow bordering The Savill Garden to the right. At the fence corner, bear right and then go right again, along a surfaced path **D**, still with The Savill Garden on the right.

Take the next path on the left and immediately bear left again. The path now passes through an area of small maple trees, which put on a glorious

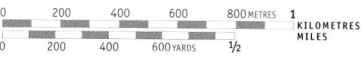

display of colour in the autumn. When the path splits, bear right, passing through an area planted with an amazing array of trees. Shortly reach the edge of Baroque-styled Cow Pond, restored in 2012. Walk with the water on the right for about 100 yards and then turn left **E**.

Keep forward to turn left upon reaching an asphalt drive, used by only the occasional vehicle. Continue straight on after passing through the Cumberland Gate **F**. The drive now passes along the edge of the huge Smith's Lawn. At the corner of the Guards' Polo Club perimeter fence **G**, turn right – heading downhill. Follow the lane over the causeway between two arms of Virginia Water and immediately turn left, between wooden bollards. Keep left along the pedestrian path. Near Temple Bungalow, go straight over two track crossings to maintain the same line as before, walking roughly parallel with the lane over to the right. Join this lane to cross the bridge over Virginia Water and then bear left **H** along the lakeside trail.

Near the mobile café, go through the gates on the left and keep right when the path immediately splits. This returns the route to the wooden gate leading back into the car park where the walk started.

The Cascade, an ornamental waterfall in Windsor Great Park

Devil's Punchbowl

walk 16

Start
Sparsholt Firs, almost 4 miles (6.3km) south-west of Wantage, Oxfordshire

Distance
6½ miles (10.4km)

Height gain
375 feet (115m)

Approximate time
3 hours

Route terrain
Grassy and stony tracks; short section on road

Parking
Sparsholt Firs car park on B4001

Dog friendly
This is a dog-friendly walk

OS maps
Landranger 174 (Newbury & Wantage), Explorer 170 (Vale of White Horse)

GPS waypoints
- SU 343 850
- Ⓐ SU 347 846
- Ⓑ SU 370 840
- Ⓒ SU 366 829
- Ⓓ SU 348 816
- Ⓔ SU 346 822
- Ⓕ SU 341 845

This is another of several routes in this book that take in part of the Ridgeway as it passes along the top of the northern edge of the North Wessex Downs. The views seem to go on forever as you follow this chalk track past the dramatic sweep of the Devil's Punchbowl. In summer, butterflies flit from one wildflower to the next, while birds sing out from the trees and hedgerows. Much of the walk is on byways, so you'll probably be sharing it with cyclists and horse riders – potentially lots of them on sunny weekends.

Take the rough, chalky track at the end of the car park furthest from the road. This is the Ridgeway. There are a couple of Ridgeway noticeboards at the start of it as well as a sign indicating that it is a 'restricted byway'. Where the clear track bends left, keep straight on.

> **The Ridgeway** This 87-mile (139-km) National Trail runs from near the massive stone circle at Avebury in Wiltshire to Ivinghoe Beacon in the Chilterns. For much of its distance, it follows an ancient thoroughfare used by prehistoric traders, invading armies and medieval herdsman to cross the chalk uplands of southern England.

About 600 yards from the car park, you'll see a fingerpost to the right of the track Ⓐ. A short detour on the path across the field to the left offers a look down into the Devil's Punchbowl. There are other views of this dry valley from further along the Ridgeway, but this is the only opportunity to get up close and personal with it. It's just 300 yards there and back to the gate above the impressive amphitheatre.

After the detour, continue along the Ridgeway in the same direction as before. As the route passes over Warren Down, there are extensive views to the north-east, but keep an eye on the area immediately to the right too as there's a good chance of seeing horses in training on the gallops. Watch too for siskins in the hawthorn trees as well as chalk-loving wildflowers such as bird's-foot trefoil.

Where the Ridgeway crosses a surfaced lane Ⓑ, turn right. The lane becomes rougher underfoot after it passes the gate of Flint Barn. Where the clear track bends right towards Cockleberry Farm, keep straight on, heading steadily downhill.

In another 500 yards, watch carefully for a sign on the left indicating to those travelling in the opposite direction that this is a restricted byway. Just 50 yards beyond this, turn right along a grassy track between the hedges **C**. The start of it is obscured by long grass in the summer, so it's easy to overlook this turning. The track dips and then climbs. Carry on to walk beside a surfaced driveway, later ignoring another lane to the left.

On reaching the barn at the top of the rise **D**, turn right. At the far side of this parking area, there is another surfaced lane. Look to the immediate left of this to identify a grassy track running parallel with the lane. Take this. (Again, this might be difficult to make out in summer because of the long grass.)

Reaching the next set of buildings, cross the driveway **E** and continue along the grassed-over byway. Later, there's nothing dividing the byway from the surfaced lane, but walkers are requested to stay on the grass. Continue to reach the B4001 road **F**, turn right and walk along the grass verge. The car park where the walk started is over to the right just after the road bends right. ●

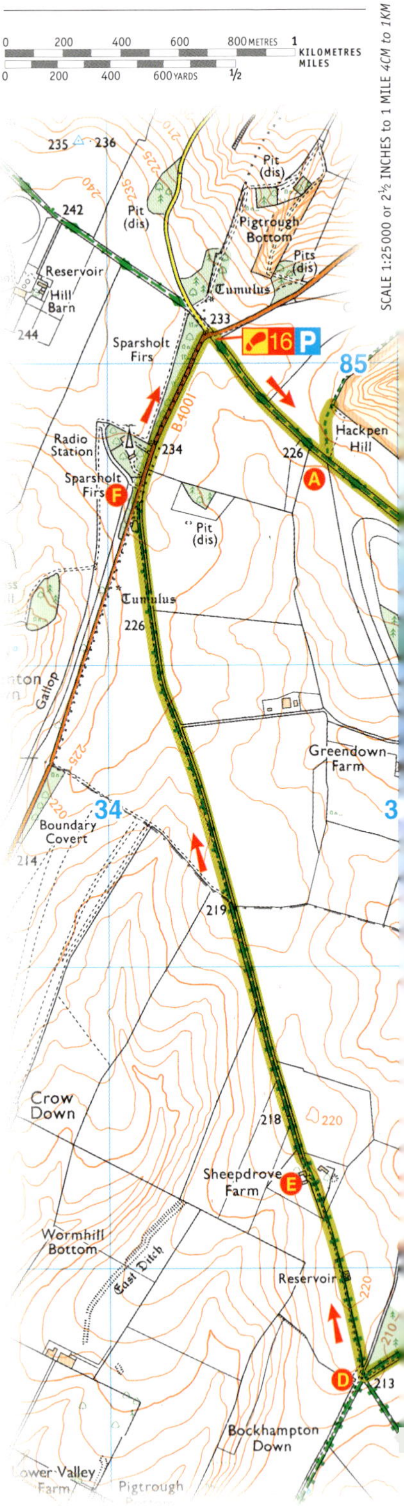

The Ridgeway is popular with horse riders

48 ● WALK 16

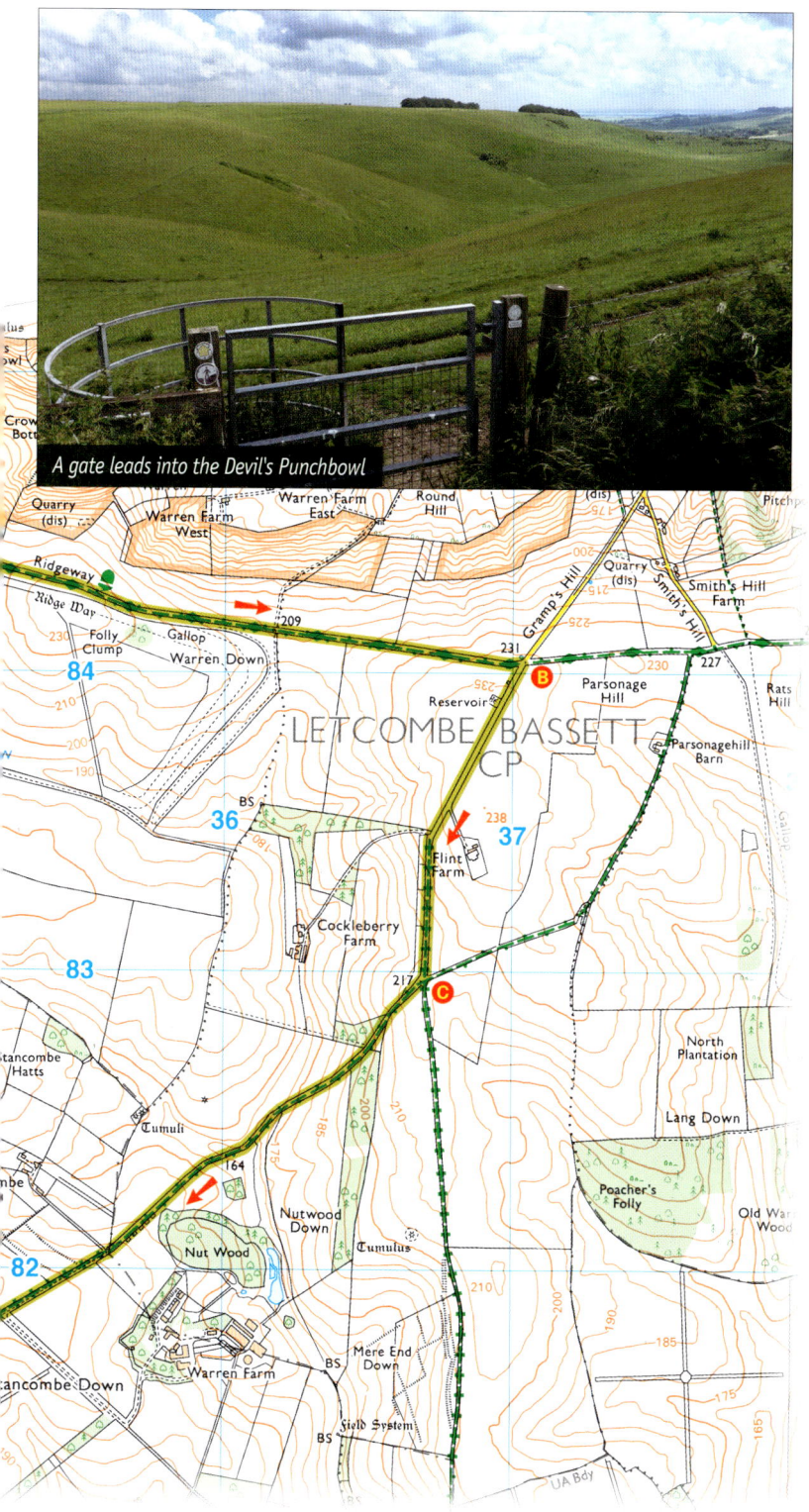

A gate leads into the Devil's Punchbowl

DEVIL'S PUNCHBOWL • 49

walk 17

Claydon House

Start
Claydon House, south-east of Steeple Claydon, Buckinghamshire

Distance
6½ miles (10.6km)

Height gain
285 feet (85m)

Approximate time
3 hours

Route terrain
Roads; farm and woodland tracks; field paths; parkland

Parking
Laybys to west of Claydon House's South Lodge on north side of minor road, ¾ mile (1.3km) west of Botolph Claydon

Dog friendly
This is a dog-friendly walk, but dogs should be on leads through the parkland

OS maps
Landranger 165 (Aylesbury & Leighton Buzzard), Explorer 192 (Buckingham & Milton Keynes)

GPS waypoints
- SP 718 249
- Ⓐ SP 708 238
- Ⓑ SP 718 224
- Ⓒ SP 727 234
- Ⓓ SP 733 245
- Ⓔ SP 736 256
- Ⓕ SP 723 258
- Ⓖ SP 719 254

This easy-going walk culminates in a visit to Claydon House, where Florence Nightingale spent several summers. To reach the 18th-century mansion, you first wind your way along country lanes, in and out of woodland and across fields that, in the summer sun, seem almost to glow with the gold of the wheat and barley. The route also passes through the charming villages of Botolph Claydon and East Claydon, both of which feature in the Domesday Book and are now home to some gorgeous cottages, typical of the settlements seen on walks throughout this book.

With your back to the laybys on the north side of the road, turn right and walk along the asphalt for ⅓ mile (525m). Take the next turning on the left – a rough lane. Nearing the buildings at Knowlhill Farm, bear left along a broad, stony track Ⓐ. Continue into the woods and, at a more open area, keep left along the well-used track. As the route approaches Finemerehill House, it splits. Bear left here. This is roughly the highest point on the walk, with far-reaching vistas to the south.

Just before the track enters a field, turn sharp left through a gate Ⓑ. Follow the path between dense hedgerows. Heading out into the open again, bear left along a track skirting the edge of the ancient woodland of Runt's Wood. Watch for bluebells and primroses in the spring. At a T-junction of tracks, go right and then, in about 65 yards, take the signposted footpath through the gap in the hedges on the left Ⓒ. Walk with the field boundary immediately on the left for 700 yards. Then look out for a fence running perpendicular to the footpath. About 40 yards beyond this, as the field boundary swings slightly left, keep straight on – through the middle of the field and aiming slightly right of the big house ahead. On the far side of the field, go through the gap in the hedgerow straight ahead, now aiming directly for the house.

SCALE 1:25 000 or $2\frac{1}{2}$ INCHES to 1 MILE 4CM to 1KM

The footpath then passes to the right of the building. Walk through the double gates to follow a rough lane between a duck pond (left) and a lovely old cottage (right).

At the road junction **D** in Botolph Claydon, cross over and turn right along the pavement, heading in almost the same direction as before – towards East Claydon. Pass the parish hall, a memorial clock tower and an unusual,

0 200 400 600 800 METRES 1 KILOMETRES
0 200 400 600 YARDS ½ MILES

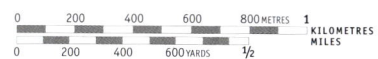

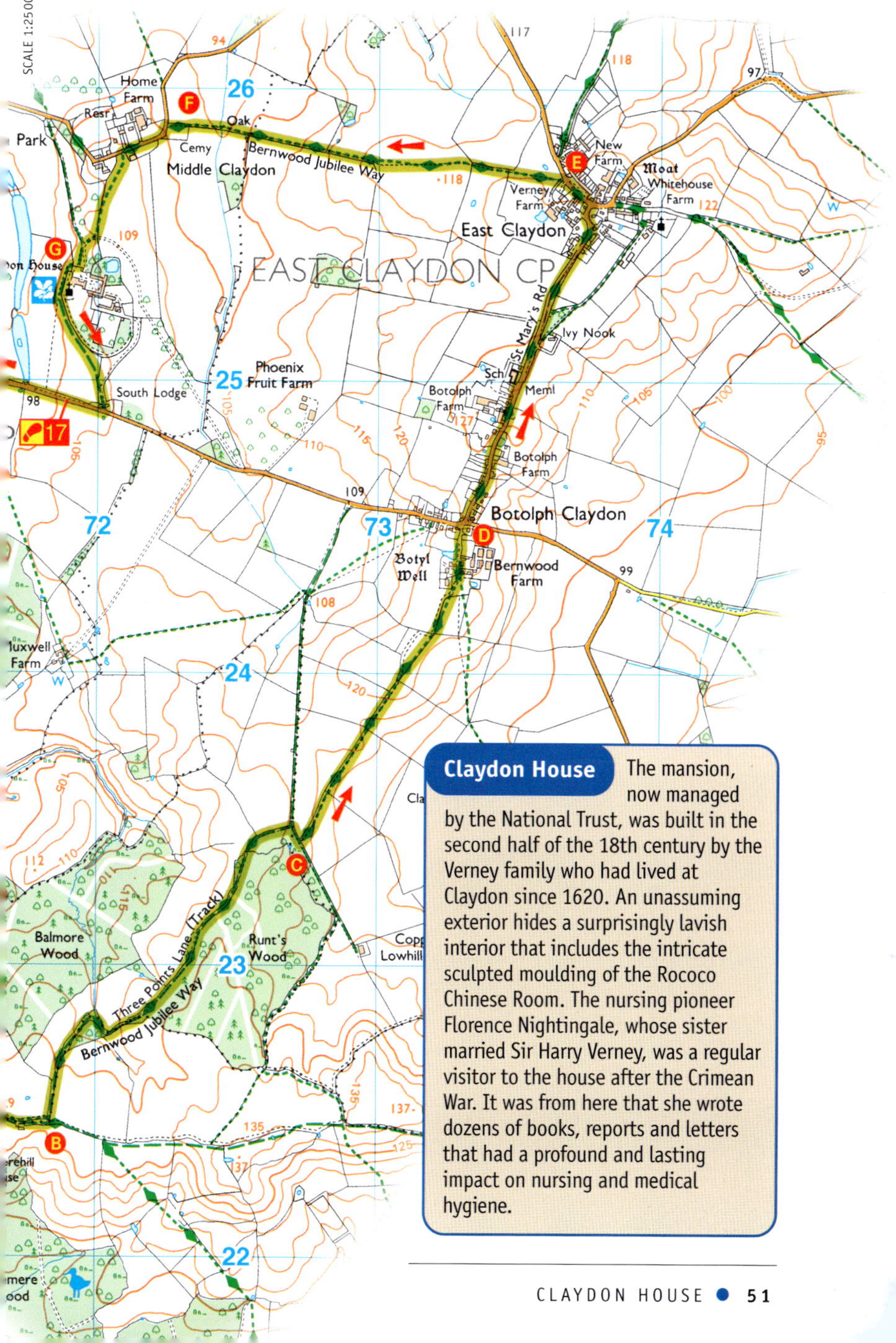

Claydon House

The mansion, now managed by the National Trust, was built in the second half of the 18th century by the Verney family who had lived at Claydon since 1620. An unassuming exterior hides a surprisingly lavish interior that includes the intricate sculpted moulding of the Rococo Chinese Room. The nursing pioneer Florence Nightingale, whose sister married Sir Harry Verney, was a regular visitor to the house after the Crimean War. It was from here that she wrote dozens of books, reports and letters that had a profound and lasting impact on nursing and medical hygiene.

Approaching Botolph Claydon

thatched shelter built around a massive tree trunk.

At the road junction in East Claydon, turn left along Sandhills Road. A little less than 150 yards beyond the junction, go through the metal kissing-gate beside a track on the left **E**. Follow a faint, grassy trail roughly west across the field. After the next gate, walk with the field boundary immediately on the right to yet another gate. Beyond this, cut straight across the middle of the field, continuing in the same direction as before. On the far side, bear right – walking with some trees and then a hedgerow on the left. The track goes from grass to stone. Having followed it for almost ½ mile (800m), go through a kissing-gate hidden in the trees on the left **F**. Rather surprisingly, the way is now through a small graveyard. Keep to the right-hand edge and exit via another gate.

Turn left to walk along the road for 200 yards. Go through a gate on the left near a small postbox and then, with the chimneys of Claydon House visible ahead, follow the line of the field boundary on the right for 300 yards. Go through a gate at a kink in the fence and drop right to reach Claydon House's public access lane. (Be careful to use the gate as there is an electric fence nearby.) Bear left along the lane and immediately fork right. (The left fork leads into the house's courtyard which is home to the **Phoenix Kitchen** café.) Nearing the house itself, bear right across a patch of gravel and then grass to a gate **G**. Once through this, swing left to pass in front of Claydon House and All Saints' Church. When the low, curving wall on the left is replaced by a wire fence, keep straight ahead making for a gate. Just beyond this, bear right along the access lane and pass between the South Lodge buildings. Turn right along the road to return to the laybys on your right in 100 yards. ●

Claydon House

Bucklebury Common

This walk explores the woods and heathland of an unfrequented area of Berkshire. Although it largely follows byways and bridleways, it also winds its way along quiet lanes that lead to out-of-the-way hamlets and pretty cottages. You'd never realise you were just outside of Thatcham – and only a few miles from the M4. This figure-of-eight walk can be cut short at **C***, reducing the total distance to 3½ miles (5.6km).*

On Bucklebury Common

From the far end of the car park, follow the narrow trail through the trees to a track. Head left and take the left-hand option. After 200 yards, follow the path on the left. Go left at a surfaced driveway and, in a few yards, turn right along the signposted byway. At the next junction, go straight across, ignoring two tracks to the left and one to the right. At the road, turn right and then left along a byway signposted to Scotland Corner. Stay left at a fork and then, at a junction in front of a cottage, go left again **A**.

Take the left-hand options at two forks in quick succession. These are soon followed by a crossing of routes. For more than ½ mile (about 1km), keep straight ahead, following the clearest path as it makes its way south-west across the common, accompanied by power lines for much of the way. When faced with a fork **B**, bear right, parting company with the power lines. Go straight over a quiet lane. Keep straight ahead until reaching a road junction. Turn right along a 'Bucklebury quiet lane' (not the main road). At a road junction next to a small cemetery **C**, turn right. This point will be returned to later in the walk.

When the lane bends left, take the track on the right and immediately turn left along a bridleway to enter a quieter part

---

walk 18

Start
Bucklebury Common, Berkshire

Distance
6½ miles (10.6km)

Height gain
300 feet (90m)

Approximate time
3 hours

Route terrain
Woodland tracks and paths, muddy in places; quiet lanes

Parking
Lower Common car park (height barrier) on south side of Broad Lane, 3¼ miles (5.2km) north-east of Thatcham

Dog friendly
Yes, but keep dogs on lead on commons during nesting season

OS maps
Landranger 174 (Newbury & Wantage), Explorer 158 (Newbury and Hungerford)

GPS waypoints
- SU 560 692
- **A** SU 565 697
- **B** SU 556 691
- **C** SU 545 688
- **D** SU 537 696
- **E** SU 532 700
- **F** SU 538 690
- **G** SU 547 686

of the woods. At a track junction near some cottages, turn right. Go diagonally left at a road crossing. Keep straight on, ignoring another bridleway to the left. About 120 yards from the road, reach an area of beech trees. The bridleway swings down to the left here; don't be tempted to keep straight on. Ignore any footpaths to the left and keep to the bridleway. On reaching a track, go straight over and then, 200 yards later, turn left along a signposted bridleway **D**.

About 100 yards after crossing another 'quiet lane', bear right (north-west) at a fork and continue in the same direction after dropping onto a wider path. Go left at a track, straight over the track in front of Slade Farm and then walk with a fence on the right. Having climbed to a lane, turn right and then take the next road on the left. In a further 250 yards, turn left along a gravel drive for about 65 yards and then bear right **E** through the grass. Staying close to the trees on the right, soon reach a complicated fingerpost. Keep straight ahead picking up a clearer path heading into the woods. Just a few strides short of a surfaced lane, turn left along a badly rutted byway. Maintain a straight line for 175 yards until nearly at the main road. Bear left along the bridleway. After just 90 yards, take the easy-to-miss turning on the left, and then keep right at a fork.

Cross a lane and ignore a bridleway to the left. Go straight over the next lane, choosing the left-hand option as the route ahead splits. After crossing a track, the path bends left. Turn left along the road **F**. Turn right at the first crossing of lanes and straight over at the second one, soon passing some pretty cottages. As the lane bends right, this part of the figure-of-eight loop is completed, returning to the point at which the quieter part of the woods was entered earlier. Retrace outward steps for 200 yards, but then keep straight on at the small cemetery **G** over to the left.

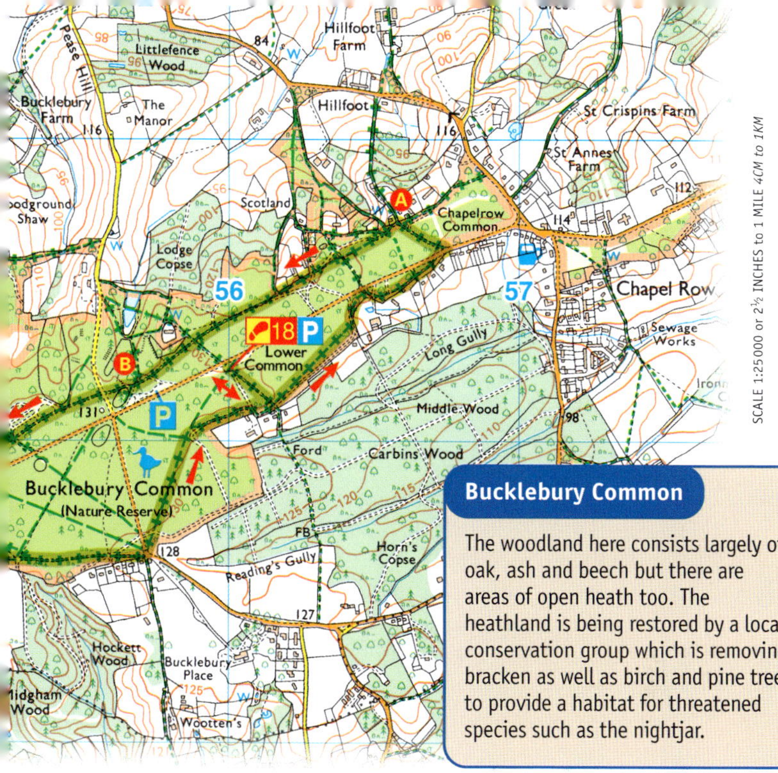

Bucklebury Common

The woodland here consists largely of oak, ash and beech but there are areas of open heath too. The heathland is being restored by a local conservation group which is removing bracken as well as birch and pine trees to provide a habitat for threatened species such as the nightjar.

0 200 400 600 800 METRES 1 KILOMETRES
0 200 400 600 YARDS ½ MILES

Go straight over at the main road and then take the byway signposted to the left **G**. Turn right along a broader path. Go straight over a track crossing. At a surfaced driveway, turn left. Cross the road and follow the muddy byway opposite. This soon becomes firmer underfoot and crosses a track to continue on to open heathland. Go straight over one gravel lane and left along the second one. The trail leading back into the car park is on the right just before the road.

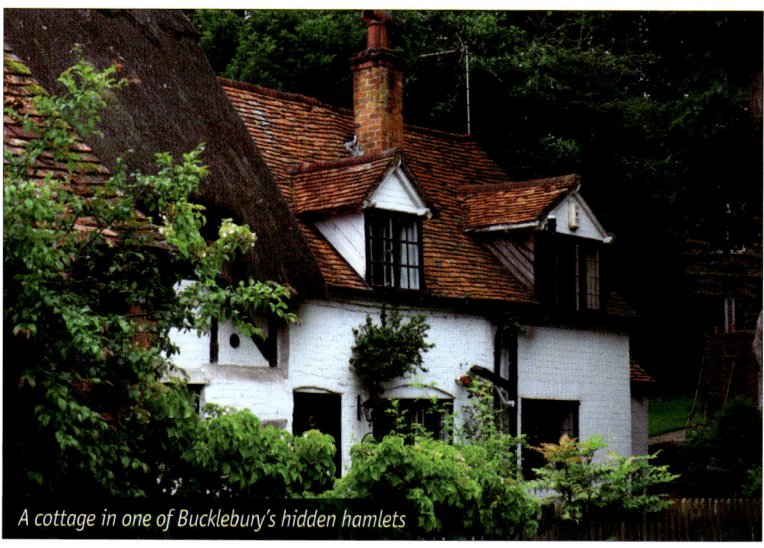

A cottage in one of Bucklebury's hidden hamlets

walk 19

Badbury Hill and Great Coxwell

Start
Badbury Hill, near Great Coxwell, Oxfordshire

Distance
6½ miles (10.6km)

Height gain
510 feet (155m)

Approximate time
3 hours

Route terrain
Field paths; village; quiet lanes; woodland

Parking
National Trust car park at Badbury Hill on B4019, 1½ miles (2.4km) east of Faringdon

Dog friendly
Two awkward stiles where dogs may need lifting (at **B** and between **C** and **D**)

OS maps
Landranger 163 (Cheltenham & Cirencester), Explorer 170 (Vale of White Horse)

GPS waypoints
- SU 261 945
- **A** SU 269 940
- **B** SU 255 933
- **C** SU 243 940
- **D** SU 254 959
- **E** SU 262 952
- **F** SU 257 945

The highlight of this walk is the village of Great Coxwell, with its impressive tithe barn, picturesque cottages and ancient church, but there's lots else besides. Distant views come and go, including the North Wessex Downs and, on a clear day, the Uffington White Horse cut into the chalk hillside. There are also a couple of gorgeous stretches of National Trust mixed woodland – Cuckoopen Plantation and Coxwell Wood. The car park itself is located next to an Iron Age site with links to the legend of King Arthur.

> **Great Coxwell Barn** This cavernous tithe barn, 144 feet (44m) long and more than 36 feet (11m) wide, was built by Cistercian monks linked with Beaulieu Abbey. It would've stored crops, including the tithes received from the abbey's peasant tenants. Using timbers in the structure's roof, dendrochronologists have been able to calculate that it was built in 1292 or soon after. Now managed by the National Trust, it is open to the public.

Head towards the car park's vehicle entrance and there see a path signposted to Great Coxwell on the left. Go through the gap in the hedge here, turn right and walk along the field edge for almost 250 yards, taking in some far-reaching views to the north along the way. At the next signpost turn right, cross the road and climb the stile next to the double gates opposite. Keep straight on, having traded a north-facing vista for views of the North Wessex Downs to the south. After a

Great Coxwell

downhill stretch, swing left and go through a metal kissing-gate. Walk with the field boundary on the left, later following it round to the right. Go through the next metal kissing-gate on

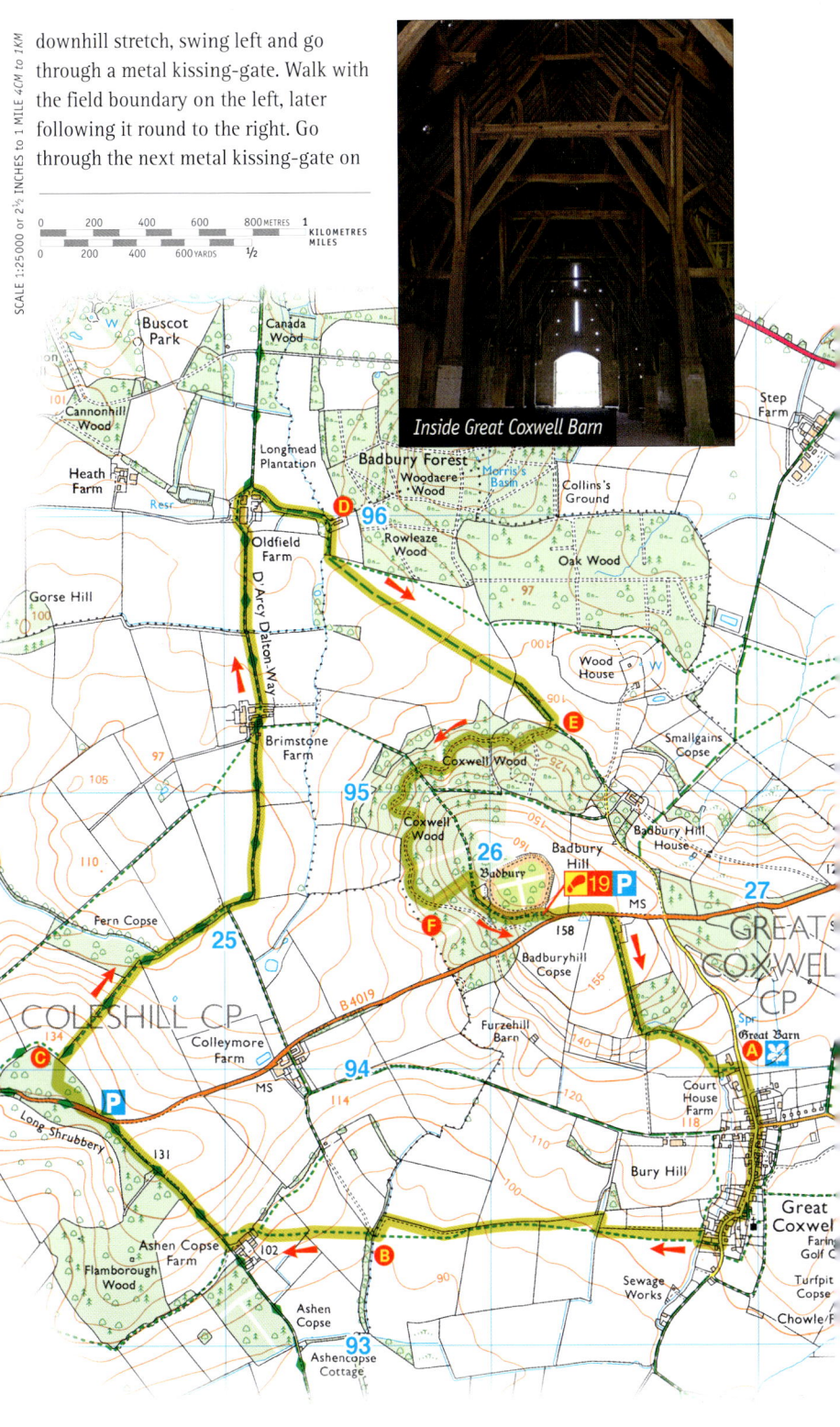

Inside Great Coxwell Barn

BADBURY HILL AND GREAT COXWELL

the left to reach Great Coxwell Barn. Pass to the right of the restored building and out on to the road **A**.

Turn right to walk through the peaceful village of Great Coxwell. There's a surfaced track to the left in 500 yards leading to the village church should you wish to visit this attractive building; otherwise keep to the road for another 250 yards and then take the gravel track on the right, signposted Coleshill. The right of way narrows and goes through a metal kissing-gate. Turn right and then, just before the next gate, left along the field edge. In a short while, if conditions are clear, the Uffington White Horse should be discernable in the distance, behind left. Beyond a gate, again go right and then left to keep to the edge of this field and the next. The path then becomes more track-like. Follow it round to the left. When it then bends right, cross the stile and bridge on the left **B**. Leave this narrow strip of trees via a gate and walk through the middle of the field. Crossing into another field, aim to the right of the buildings at Ashen Copse Farm. At the shed corner, bear left. Reaching the far end of these buildings, turn right along a concrete track and then right along the access lane.

Go left along the B4019. At the layby to the right of the road, go through the gap between the trees to enter Cuckoopen Plantation. Head into the woods on a faint trail and then turn left along a wider path. Just a few strides short of a split in the route ahead, turn sharp right along an easy-to-miss trail that winds its way to the north-eastern edge of the woods. Step out on to the farmland at a waymarker post **C** next to a tall hedgerow. Head to the right of the hedgerow and follow it downhill. Cross the stile at the bottom of the slope and continue along the field edge in the same direction as before.

Turn left along a surfaced lane and follow it to Brimstone Farm. On entering the farmyard, swing right on a concrete track between the buildings. The track leads to Oldfield Farm. Here, keep to the left of the buildings. Once past them – as the surfaced lane swings left – keep straight on to follow a rough track. At first, there's a hedgerow on the left and another farm shed over to the right. The track ends near a row of isolated cottages **D**.

Go through a gate here and keep straight on, along the field edge. After the next gate, the bridleway cuts diagonally left through the middle of an enormous field. (Alternatively, you can follow the permanent grass strip around the left-hand side of the field.) On the far (eastern) side of the field, go through a gate with several National Trust waymarkers on it and then use the strip of sparsely placed trees to guide progress south-east. Go through a gate **E** to enter Coxwell Wood and follow the clearest path (right) into the trees. After about 100 yards, turn right along a wider, often muddier path. Thankfully, it quickly becomes more solid underfoot. Go straight over at a waymarked crossing of routes. Follow this meandering path for a further 700 yards – another trail joining from the left along the way. At a staggered crossing of paths **F**, turn left, heading steeply uphill. Go right at the next junction to visit Badbury Clumps Iron Age fort on the left just before re-entering the car park. ●

> **Badbury Clumps** This Iron Age fort is thought to have been the site of a battle in about the fifth century AD between native Celts, supposedly led by King Arthur, and Anglo-Saxons.

Deddington and the Oxford Canal

The medieval market town of Deddington lies to the south of Banbury, close to Oxfordshire's border with Northamptonshire. In fact, this walk briefly crosses into the neighbouring county after sampling some of the pleasant farm paths and bridleways to the south-west of the village and then enjoying a spell beside the Oxford Canal. After passing through the attractive village of Clifton, a series of farm tracks leads back to Deddington and an opportunity to visit the substantial earthwork remains of its Norman castle.

walk 20

Start
Old Town Hall in Deddington, Oxfordshire

Distance
8 miles (12.9km)

Height gain
270 feet (80m)

Approximate time
3½ hours

Route terrain
Farm tracks; field paths; canal towpath; roadside path

Parking
Roadside parking in centre of Deddington

Dog friendly
One awkward stile where dogs may need lifting **E**

OS maps
Landranger 151 (Stratford-upon-Avon), Explorer 191 (Banbury, Bicester & Chipping Norton)

GPS waypoints
- SP 467 316
- **A** SP 475 306
- **B** SP 486 301
- **C** SP 492 291
- **D** SP 496 290
- **E** SP 498 314
- **F** SP 493 318
- **G** SP 469 316

Standing with your back to the Old Town Hall in Deddington, there are two roads to the right. Ignore the one heading past the **Unicorn Inn**; instead, take the one running almost parallel to the Old Town Hall. This soon narrows and then bends left. On the bend, turn right along Philcote Street (later St Thomas Street). Go left at the A4260 and almost immediately left again along Chapmans Lane. Beyond the last of the houses, the surfaced lane becomes a rough track. This winds its way down to the farm buildings at Leadenporch **A**. Go left along the surfaced track and turn right at the T-junction. When the surfaced lane then bends right to enter a private courtyard, continue straight ahead – with the paddock fence on the left at first. The bridleway soon cuts a grassy swathe through the field.

> **Deddington Castle** Odo, Bishop of Bayeux and half-brother of William the Conqueror, had this motte-and-bailey castle built in the 11th century. Although no stonework is visible today, the earthworks are substantial – almost 50 feet (15m) high in places. Tree-covered, they enclose a flat, grassy area covering 7½ acres (3 hectares).

At a junction with another broad path, turn right and then go left on entering a field. Beyond the gate in the corner, cut straight across the next field – walking in the same direction as before. After the next gate, veer slightly right (east-south-east). On the far side of the field, follow the hedgerow down into a dip. As a bridleway goes left, veer right, crossing Bowman's Bridge **B**. Follow the clear path round to the right and through a farm gate. Turn left along the field edge. Go through a double gate and continue along the field's left-hand edge. After the

DEDDINGTON AND THE OXFORD CANAL • 59

Cruising on the Oxford Canal

next gate, keep to the right of a clump of bushes straight ahead to locate another set of gates. Once through these, continue beside the fence on the left. Nearing Mill Cottage, swing right, go through the bridle gate and turn left along the road **C**.

The road crosses a mill race (watch for some beautifully converted mill buildings on the right here) and the River Cherwell. Just before the third bridge – over the Oxford Canal at Somerton – take the trail on the left, quickly joining the towpath **D**. Now walk with the waterway, keeping it to the right, for the next 1¾ miles (3km), passing Somerton Lock along the way and, hopefully, a few colourful canal boats too. Soon after drawing level with the buildings at Wharf Farm on the other side of the water, spot a bridge ahead. Just before the canal passes under the bridge, leave the towpath by crossing the stile to the left **E**.

Turn left along the track. When it ends, go through the gate and walk beside the fence on the right. When the fence kinks right, maintain the same line, aiming for a wooden gate ahead. Once through this, go straight across the next field. After a gated bridge, veer half-right, aiming for the metal gate about 100 yards right of the converted mill. Once through this, turn left along the B4031 **F**. Walk through Clifton and, nearing the far side of the village, turn right along Tithe Lane. Ignoring County View to the left, keep straight ahead. Beyond Hazel Head Cottage, the track passes a barrier and enters the fields. At the next track junction, turn left along a permissive footpath. At the top of the rise, follow this stony track to the left and then to the right at the next junction. It becomes a sealed lane at the next group of buildings. In another ¼ mile (400m), at a set of signs, turn right through the gap in the hedges and then walk south-south-west through the middle of two fields.

The path comes out at Earl's Lane, close to its junction with the B4031. Turn right along the main road. In another 230 yards, watch for a narrow

The village of Clifton

lane on the left – beside Castle Lodge **G**. This leads down to the site of Deddington Castle. Having visited the castle, head back to the road and turn left, continuing into Deddington. Coming to Philcote Street on the left, follow the main road round to the right. The Old Town Hall is soon in sight over on the left.

DEDDINGTON AND THE OXFORD CANAL • 61

walk 21 *Waddesdon*

Start
Waddesdon, Buckinghamshire

Distance
7 miles (11.3km)

Height gain
310 feet (95m)

Approximate time
3¼ hours

Route terrain
Quiet lane; woodland; parkland; field paths; pavement through village

Parking
Layby on south side of A41 on eastern edge of Waddesdon

Dog friendly
Awkward stiles where dogs may need lifting – just before **E** and at **B** for those wanting to detour to St Mary Magdalene Church

OS maps
Landranger 165 (Aylesbury & Leighton Buzzard), Explorers 180 (Oxford) and 181 (Chiltern Hills North)

GPS waypoints
- SP 749 168
- **A** SP 743 163
- **B** SP 745 144
- **C** SP 731 152
- **D** SP 720 164
- **E** SP 718 170
- **F** SP 733 170
- **G** SP 739 169

The Buckinghamshire village of Waddesdon is dominated by the presence of Waddesdon Manor, the château-like mansion that hides in the woodland above. This walk completes a circuit of the hill on which it sits, with glimpses of the house and its parkland coming and going. The route also calls in at Upper Winchendon's St Mary Magdalene, a gloriously situated hilltop church with superb views to the west. Some of the rights of way, particularly on the first part of the walk, barely exist on the ground, so you'll need to pay extra close attention to the map and walk description.

Head to the end of the layby nearest Waddesdon and turn left along the dead-end lane. Pass to the right of the gated compound at the end of the lane - onto the Waddesdon Greenway - and immediately turn right. The clear path crosses a lane. Continue on the surfaced path until it bends sharp right. Turn left on this bend. This path later bends left to reach a crossing of routes. Turn right here - through the trees. Bending left again, the route emerges in an area of younger trees. Now veer right, with a hedgerow on the right.

Cross a surfaced track **A**, and bear slightly left (south-south-west) to walk through the long grass (no path). On the far side, reach another surfaced track. Cross this and keep forward down a private road (heading south-south-east; it has gates across it.) Soon after this road bends left, go through the pedestrian gate in the hedgerow on the right. Head straight across this first field, on a faint trail heading roughly south. Soon see a gap between two hedgerows running perpendicular to each other. Go through this and, in the next field, head for the gate in the hedges on the far side – staying on level ground. Once through, climb south-south-west for about 150 yards and then bear left, south-east. (If you look back now, you will see you are passing between rows of trees that lead up to Waddesdon Manor on top of the hill.) Watch for a clump of trees over to the right – surrounded by railings. Just after passing above it, descend the slope on the right, heading south-west to the farm gate in the field corner. Once through, walk up the field edge on the left (ignoring the ladder stile). At the top of the rise **B**, the main route goes right. For a short detour to the beautifully situated church of

> **Waddesdon Manor** Built to resemble a French château but on a massive scale, Waddesdon Manor was erected in the late 19th century for Baron Ferdinand de Rothschild. Now open to the public, it contains a significant collection of art and antiquities. The cellars, opened in 1994, contain more than 15,000 bottles of Rothschild wines.

WADDESDON • 63

Looking into the grounds of Waddesdon Manor

St Mary Magdalene, cross the stile next to the locked farm gate and turn left.

Back on the main route, walk along the top edge of the field and climb the stile next to a gate. Cross the cattle grid on the right and fork right to go through a gate. When the concrete track ends, go through the small gate and, with a super view ahead, walk along the right-hand edge of the next two fields. Maintaining the same direction, walk straight across the middle of a further two fields. On the far side of the fourth field, keep straight ahead, through a gate, and then continue beside a fence on the right. After a gate on the far side, cross the sealed farm lane **C** to join a rough track. Pass to the left of a gate across the track, but then rejoin it beyond the buildings at Westcott Field Farm.

Go straight over the road to negotiate a bridge and gate hidden by the hedgerow **D**. Look slightly right of the large shed ahead to see a gate on the far side of the field. Go through this and through an identical one on the other side of the old road. Keep the fence on the right through an open area. On the far side, go through the small gate and swing right through the trees. Emerging in another open area, look to the far side to locate a tiny gap between a wooden garden fence and a tall hedgerow to the left of it. Make for this, and then on reaching it, cross the stile. An enclosed path winds its way between the gardens.

Turn right at the road in Westcott **E** and then left along Lower Green. As the lane bends left, take the path between the houses on the right. After the metal kissing-gate, keep to the left-hand side of the field for 100 yards and then turn left through another kissing-gate. Cross the field on the diagonal, go through a gate and then maintain roughly the same bearing along a grassy strip through the middle of the next field. On the far side, keep straight ahead walking between two lines of hedgerow. Join a rough track heading in the ongoing direction. At the next junction **F**, go left and immediately right, soon walking beside some nursery glasshouses. Keep straight on at a staggered crossing of lanes. On reaching the A41 opposite **The Bow** pub **G**, turn right to walk through Waddesdon. The layby where the walk started is accessed via the lane on the right just after the national speed limit sign.

Wendover Woods

walk 22

One of the finest features of the Chiltern Hills is its beautiful deciduous woodland; and one of the best places to experience this is at Wendover Woods. This sprawling forest to the east of the pretty little town from which it takes its name is criss-crossed by miles and miles of trails, just a few of which are sampled on this delightful, undulating walk. The route also includes a section of the old towpath beside the now disused Wendover Arm of the Grand Union Canal.

Start
Wendover Woods Café next to car park, Buckinghamshire

Distance
6¾ miles (11km)

Height gain
920 feet (280m)

Approximate time
3½ hours

Route terrain
Forest tracks and trails; canal towpath; short section on road; golf course

Parking
Forestry England's main Wendover Woods car park

Dog friendly
This is a dog-friendly walk

OS maps
Landranger 165 (Aylesbury & Leighton Buzzard), Explorer 181 (Chiltern Hills North)

GPS waypoints
- SP 889 089
- Ⓐ SP 892 074
- Ⓑ SP 884 082
- Ⓒ SP 883 100
- Ⓓ SP 879 106
- Ⓔ SP 889 109
- Ⓕ SP 891 101

With your back to the main entrance to the **café**, turn right, very soon passing the public toilets. Take the next path on the right. This marks the start of the waymarked Firecrest Trail. Keep straight on, always following the clearest path – even when the Firecrest Trail heads right after a few hundred yards. This part of the walk takes place under a gorgeous beech canopy.

Keep straight on at a crossing of routes. The path ahead, on grass now, soon swings right. Beyond the barrier and stile, aim for the house and then follow the line of its driveway. Just a few strides short of the road, go through the gap in the hedges on the right Ⓐ. Continue with hedges to the left, walking parallel with the road until the next set of houses. Immediately after these, take the track on the right. Coming to a barrier, take the public right of way a few yards to the left – through a gap in some railings. After the next set of railings, bear left along a clearer path, still climbing steadily. The gradient eases after

Seating outside the Wendover Woods Café

another broad path joins from the left. There is a junction of paths at the top of the climb **B**. The Iron Age Boddington hillfort is just to the left here, but our route continues on the far side of the small, grass mound that has a solitary tree growing from it.

After about 350 yards, bear right at an obvious fork. An open area with a bench soon provides great views to the west, while the toposcope helps visitors identify distant landmarks. All the while, steadily lose height, with the descent steepening after another path joins from the right. After two barriers in quick succession, keep straight ahead. Carefully cross the busy B4009 **C** and take the lane opposite. This area is part of the MoD's Halton Camp, one of the largest RAF bases in England at the time of writing, although its phased closure was about to begin. Immediately after passing a lane turning on the right, turn right along a path on the far side of some bollards. The shady route ahead is lined by a range of trees including yews, one of the UK's three native conifer species. Briefly brush up against a surfaced lane. At this point, turn sharp right to re-enter the woods. Just before some concrete obstructions, head left on a less obvious trail. Bear right at a fork near the canal and, almost immediately, bear left at a waymarker post. Turn right along the canal towpath **D**.

The arboreal theme of the walk continues, with the canal fringed on both sides by deciduous species. Watch for the blue flash of kingfishers darting along the bank, particularly near Wellonhead Bridge. Immediately after passing under this bridge, the second on this ¾-mile (1.2-km) stroll along the towpath, take the path on the right (beside the steps). Part of the Outer Aylesbury Ring long-distance route, this soon joins Stablebridge Road, along which turn left.

Carefully re-cross the B4009 and go through the pedestrian gate opposite **E**. Reaching the edge of a golf course, aim for a small building up to the right. Take the track from here, along the top edge of the course. Just before it enters the car park, follow the line of white posts straight ahead and round the side of the clubhouse. The final post marks the spot at which the footpath re-enters forestry land. After a steady climb, turn right at a track junction.

Turn left at the road **F** and immediately take the footpath signposted to the right. Go right again at a track junction. At the gate into The Chalet, bear left, walking beside a fence. Keep straight on after a large gate. Just beyond a locked barrier, continue on the surfaced lane coming up from the right. Go straight over a crossing of lanes near the car park entrance and over to the left is the Wendover Woods Café and other visitor facilities. ●

Wandering the Wendover Woods

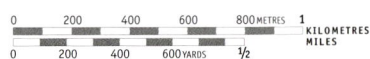

Wendover Arm of the Grand Union Canal Linking Bulbourne in Hertfordshire with Wendover in Buckinghamshire, this 6¾-mile (10.8-km) stretch of canal opened in 1799. Most of it has been unnavigable since the end of the 19th century, but the Wendover Canal Trust restored and reopened a short section in 2005. The charity aims to reopen the whole canal, and restore the towpath in its entirety, by 2030.

Longer walks of more than 3½ hours

The Column of Victory in the grounds of Blenheim Palace

Ridgeway and West Ilsley

There's lots of variety on this lovely walk on the North Wessex Downs. It starts with a stretch of the Ridgeway, a prehistoric route across the high ground that is now a National Trail. After following undulating tracks and field paths, it then calls in at the perfect Berkshire settlement of West Ilsley where you can sit outside the village pub and watch a game of cricket or enjoy a picnic beside the duck pond. The return route includes another chance to savour the distant views from the Ridgeway.

Head to the westernmost end of the two-sided car park and take the restricted byway, part of the Ridgeway National Trail, heading roughly north-west. In spring, skylarks are company on this part of the journey, jubilantly singing as they rise vertically from the long grass beside the track. Watch too for corn buntings, meadow pipits and yellowhammers. There's also a good chance of spotting red kites.

After just more than a mile (1.7km), keep left as another path goes right. The chalky track, now with chunks of flint showing through, climbs to a small parking area **A** and a junction of routes. Cross diagonally right to continue on the Ridgeway. About 125 yards beyond a second parking area among the trees, watch for a trail to the left **B**. This leads through a gate to Scutchamer Knob, but the main route continues roughly west along the Ridgeway, soon heading back out into the open again. Just after another stretch of steady ascent, there is a patch of woodland on the right. Immediately after this, turn left along a farm track **C**.

Immediately after passing through the next area of woodland, turn left **D** (south-south-east) through the field. A broad swathe is cut through the crops to enable easy passage of walkers and riders. Reaching the bottom edge of the field, continue between the trees to drop on to a byway known as Old

Scutchamer Knob

This early Iron Age barrow would once have been round, but the remaining earthworks are semi-circular in shape. The banks are obscured by vegetation in the height of summer, but visitors can still walk around the top of them.

---

walk 23

Start
Bury Down, Berkshire, 5 miles (8km) south-west of Didcot

Distance
7¾ miles (12.4km)

Height gain
510 feet (155m)

Approximate time
3¾ hours

Route terrain
Tracks; field paths; short section of road through village

Parking
Bury Down car park

Dog friendly
This is a dog-friendly walk

OS maps
Landranger 174 (Newbury & Wantage), Explorer 170 (Vale of White Horse)

GPS waypoints
- SU 479 840
- **A** SU 458 850
- **B** SU 456 850
- **C** SU 443 849
- **D** SU 444 836
- **E** SU 448 822
- **F** SU 461 827
- **G** SU 476 823
- **H** SU 486 836

Street. Bear left along this to reach the road at Lands End. Go diagonally right to continue on Old Street as it heads south.

Just over ½ mile (about 1km) beyond the road at Lands End – and at the top of an uphill stretch – turn left along a signposted bridleway **E**. The route keeps to the field edge and can be swamped by long grass and nettles in summer. At the far end of the field, go through the small wooden gate and then bear slightly right across this open area to join a clear track. This eventually becomes the access lane to the beautifully renovated Starveall Farm. Follow this towards the road, enjoying great views of the surrounding rolling farmland on the way.

A few strides short of the asphalt, look for a gap in the fence on the right **F**. Go through this and walk over to the hedgerow to follow a bridleway running down the side of the field, parallel with the road. There is an open area on the far side of the field. A gap in the hedges on the left enables you to continue in the same direction as before but now on asphalt.

Follow the road into the pretty village of West Ilsley, complete with pub, cricket pitch, duck pond, church and quaint cottages. On the far side of the village, immediately before the national speed limit sign, turn left along a restricted byway **G**. The track forks just before the last of the cottages. Keep right here, along the gently rising track. Reaching a more open area, keep to the left of the white railings marking the edge of the gallops on Hodcott Down. Before long, come to a junction with a broad, grassy track – the Ridgeway **H**. With far-reaching views of the Thames Valley to the north, turn left along the ancient trackway.

The walk re-enters the Bury Down car park via its eastern half.

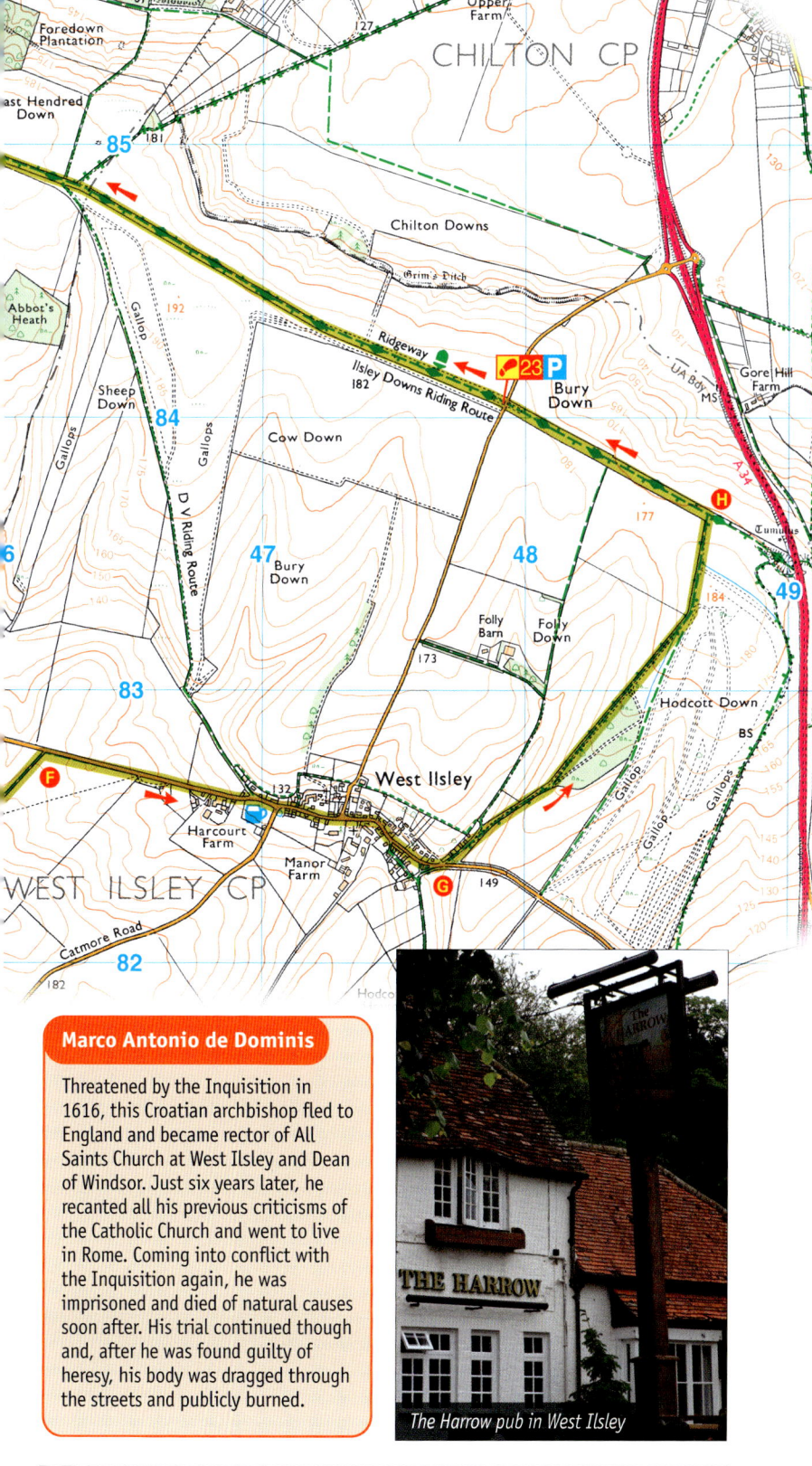

Marco Antonio de Dominis

Threatened by the Inquisition in 1616, this Croatian archbishop fled to England and became rector of All Saints Church at West Ilsley and Dean of Windsor. Just six years later, he recanted all his previous criticisms of the Catholic Church and went to live in Rome. Coming into conflict with the Inquisition again, he was imprisoned and died of natural causes soon after. His trial continued though and, after he was found guilty of heresy, his body was dragged through the streets and publicly burned.

The Harrow pub in West Ilsley

walk 24

Chalgrove

Start
Chalgrove, Oxfordshire

Distance
8 miles (12.9km)

Height gain
325 feet (100m)

Approximate time
3¾ hours

Route terrain
Field paths; roads

Parking
Village car park beside recreation area, accessed via lane down the side of The Crown pub

Dog friendly
There are eight awkward stiles

OS maps
Landranger 164 (Oxford), Explorer 171 (Chiltern Hills West)

GPS waypoints
- SU 636 968
- Ⓐ SU 627 961
- Ⓑ SU 617 962
- Ⓒ SU 611 965
- Ⓓ SU 613 955
- Ⓔ SU 623 943
- Ⓕ SU 652 949
- Ⓖ SU 643 957

This gentle farmland walk in south Oxfordshire links several attractive villages, some with lovely old churches. It starts from Chalgrove, drops in on the historic hamlet of Newington, visits tranquil Berrick Prior and then returns via the pretty Brightwell Baldwin. Time your walk carefully, and you'll also have a choice of pubs to visit.

St Mary's, Chalgrove

The nave of this 12th-century church is home to 44 exceptional wall paintings created in the 1320s and 1330s. Showing scenes from the life of Christ and the Virgin Mary, they were covered by limewash at the time of the Reformation, only to be rediscovered in the middle of the 19th century. The time of the paintings' creation coincided with a period of relative wealth for St Mary's. In 1317, Edward II granted the living of Chalgrove to Thame Abbey in return for the monks performing daily mass for the souls of his ancestors and his murdered lover Piers Gaveston. Guides lead regular tours of the church. Alternatively, visitors can get the key from the village shop.

Walk down the western side of the recreation area, passing to the right of the children's play area. Keep right along an obvious path between a fence on the left and trees on the right. After a bridge, keep straight ahead through the middle of the playing field. Beyond the gap in the hedge on the far side, continue along the field edge. Go straight over at a minor road. When the fenced section of path ends, stay with the power lines until meeting some trees at the top of the next field Ⓐ.

Don't go through the gap in the trees here; instead, turn right to walk with the field boundary on the left. The line taken along this field edge leads naturally through an arched gap in some trees. Go straight over a farm track to walk with a solar farm on the left-hand side. On the far side of this, look for a line of hedgerow slightly ahead and to the right. Stroll over to this and then walk with it on the right. The vague track underfoot splits at the far end of this short stretch of hedgerow. Bear left. About 500 yards beyond the solar farm, there is a temptation to swing left with a rough track Ⓑ, but maintain the now pathless line, walking with a field boundary on the left. Pass through the hedgerow and continue along the field edge. About 70 yards after the field boundary bends slightly right, go through an easy-to-miss gap in the vegetation on the left. A trail leads

St Giles's Church, Newington

through this uncultivated area. Cross a bridge and stile, and head west-north-west on a line through the grass. This leads to a stile ❍.

The route returns to this point after visiting Newington, which is home to the pretty church of St Giles and a 17th-century manor house. Cross this stile and a second one. Aim for the houses below, cross the stile in front of them and then follow the path to the A329. The church and manor are to the left. Having explored, return to the pair of stiles at ❍. After crossing, turn right and negotiate yet another stile. There is little to guide the way across the next area of farmland. The right-of-way goes south-south-east initially, heading towards a small copse. There is no way through the trees, so keep to the western (right-hand) edge of them. There's a grassy track here that then passes through the middle of the crops. When it later bends left, leave it by continuing roughly south. Aim to the right of a power pole almost halfway between Lane End Farm and Ewe Farm. Just beyond this, there is a trail through the vegetation at the field edge. It's not easy to spot.

Turn left along the road ❍. In Berrick Prior, take the lane on the left at the crossroads. At a sharp bend to the right ❍, follow the bridleway straight ahead – signed to Brightwell Baldwin. Go straight across at a road to continue on the bridleway. Later emerging in a field, walk with the hedgerow on the left. At a crossing of routes, keep straight on – along a rough track. On the far side of the field, keep left. Leave this broad track when it bends left. Keep straight on here, through a gate. After the next gate, walk with the fence on the right. A further gate gives access to another fenced section of bridleway. This leads to a lane **F** on the edge of Brightwell Baldwin. Turn right here and go left at the road.

The route now passes the church, surprisingly large for such a small village, and the **Lord Nelson** pub. Drawing level with thatched Glebe Farm on the right, cross the stile on the left, joining Shakespeare's Way. The path stays close to the fence on the left as it makes its way along the edge of Brightwell Park's unkempt parkland. (The unusual building on the right in a short while is a dovecote.) After another two stiles, cross a track and then follow the trail cut through the crops ahead. Beyond the next stile, aim for the large gate some way to the right of Cadwell Farm. Cross the stile next to this. The

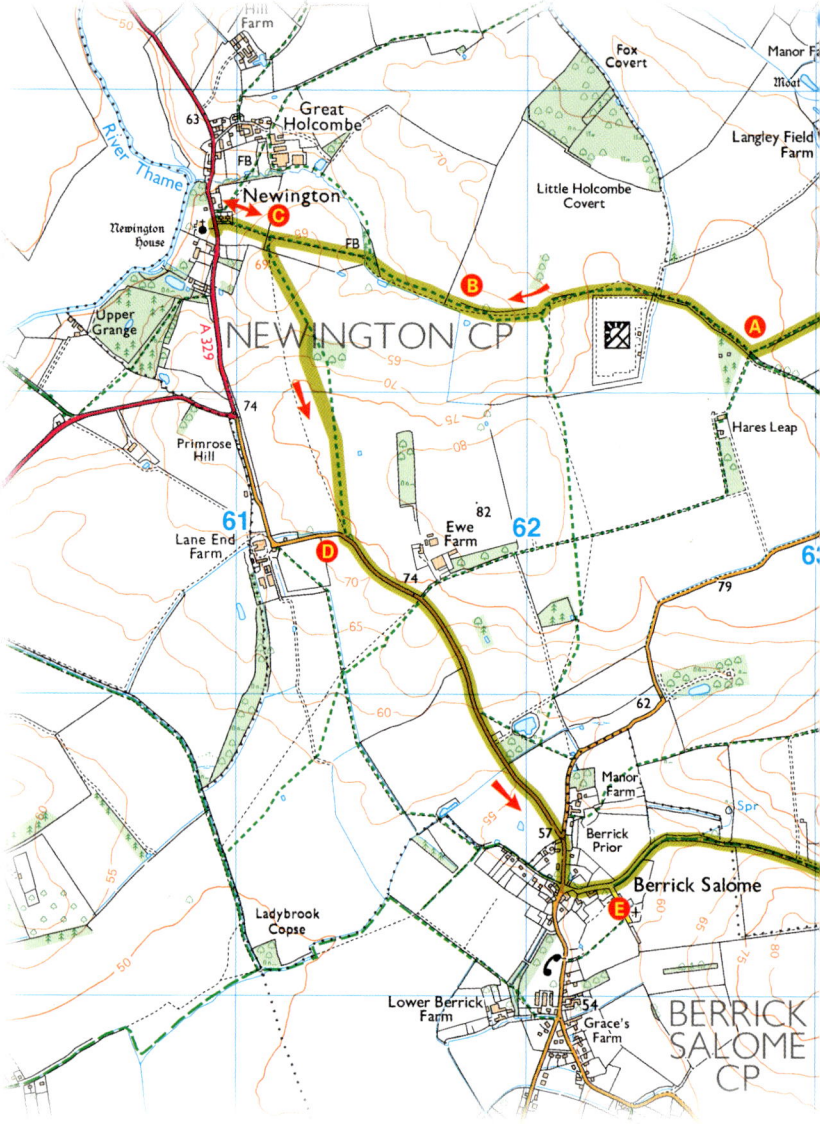

trail through the trees leads to a grassy track. Bear left here and quickly turn right along the surfaced farm lane **G**.

Later, turn right at the road. Follow it round to the left and go left at the T-junction – along High Street. Turn left again along Church Lane. The road bends right near a thatched cottage. Take the track on the left here – towards the church. Passing to the right of the church, ignore a trail heading into a residential area; keep straight on to locate a path leading back to the recreation area. Pass to the left of a tennis court and five-a-side pitch and then see, to the left, the path taken earlier. Ignoring this, keep straight on – with the play area over on the right – to return to the car park.

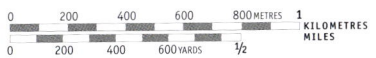

SCALE 1:25000 or 2½ INCHES to 1 MILE 4CM to 1KM

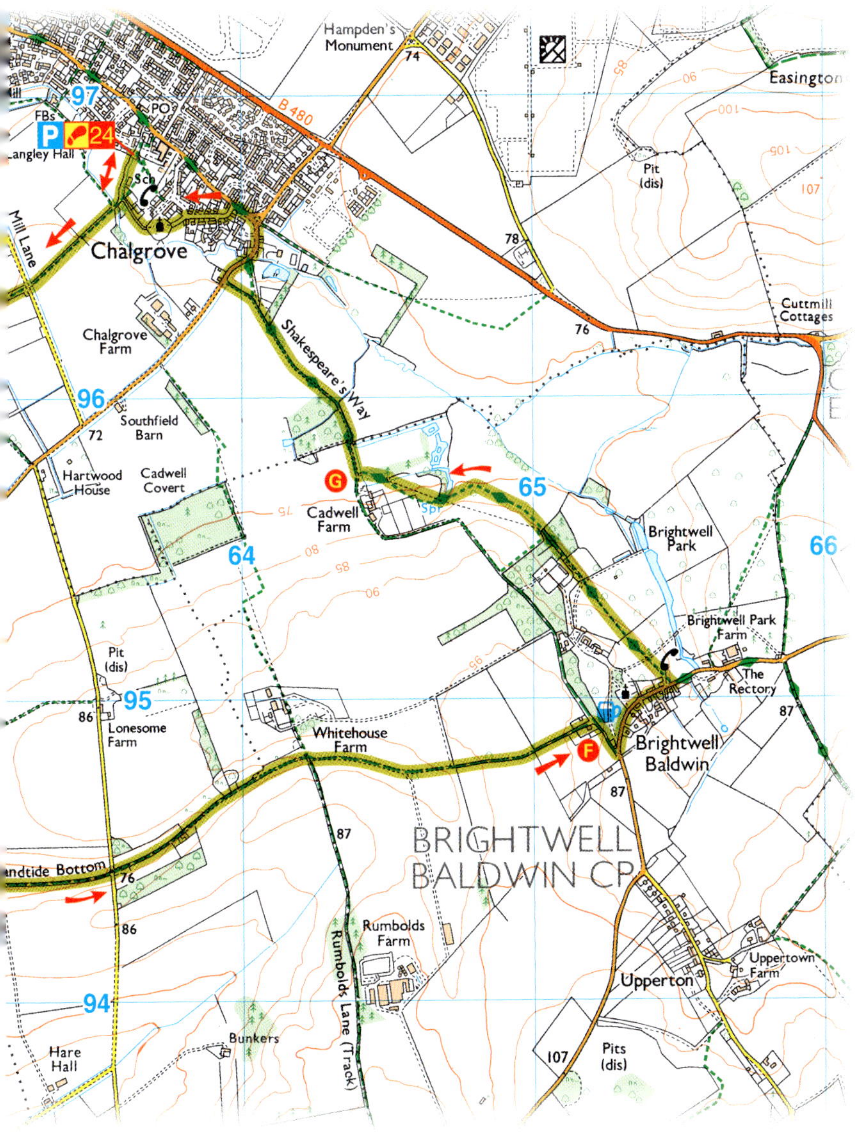

walk 25

Lambourn Downs

Start
Lambourn, Berkshire

Distance
8¾ miles (14.2km)

Height gain
570 feet (175m)

Approximate time
4¼ hours

Route terrain
Pavement through town; quiet lanes; tracks and field paths on downs

Parking
Car park on High Street, Lambourn

Dog friendly
This is a dog-friendly walk

OS maps
Landranger 174 (Newbury & Wantage), Explorer 170 (Vale of White Horse)

GPS waypoints
- SU 325 788
- Ⓐ SU 321 797
- Ⓑ SU 310 804
- Ⓒ SU 289 811
- Ⓓ SU 292 822
- Ⓔ SU 307 838
- Ⓕ SU 316 818
- Ⓖ SU 320 810

A stroll along a quiet lane lined with the idyllic thatched cottages of Upper Lambourn provides a relaxed start to this superb day on the downs of West Berkshire. A gentle climb across farmland and along chalk tracks then leads to the high ground where gentle breezes blow through fields of wheat and barley in the summer, while horses thunder along the gallops, training for the next big race. There's a wonderful sense of expansiveness as you stride out along the ridges, with big skies dominating these wide, open spaces.

Thatched cottage in Upper Lambourn

Leave the car park and turn left along High Street. Go straight over at the crossroads and then, immediately after the church, turn left along a paved walkway, keeping the church railings to the left. (The unusual-looking building on the right forms part of the Isbury Almshouses, established in 1502.) Cross Big Lane and then continue in the same direction as before – along the pavement beside Upper Lambourn Road. Having walked the pavement for 650 yards, turn right along Uplands Lane and then take the next lane on the left Ⓐ. Lined by thatched cottages and racing stables, this makes for a very pleasant start to the day. When the asphalt ends, take the surfaced path to the left of the byway straight ahead. The asphalt lane restarts a little further on, this time with a pathway to the right of it. After following this section of the lane for 750 yards, Craven Cottage appears on the right. Turn right immediately after this Ⓑ.

Initially on a surfaced track, but, maintaining the same line, soon join a bridleway. When a track crosses the right of way, keep straight on, now following a grassier route between the fields. In spring and summer, this is lined with an assortment of chalk-loving wildflowers, and, in the right conditions, there'll be dozens of butterflies flitting back and forth. Heading in the same direction all the while, join a rough track and then a surfaced lane. At a T-junction of lanes, continue straight ahead on the bridleway, grassy again. Keep to this until it reaches a broad, chalky track **C**. Now turn right.

Nearing the top of the hill, swing right, keeping the field boundary on the right. This is a particularly lovely part of the walk; you can really stride out and, at about 650 feet (200m) above sea level, take in the excellent views of the surrounding countryside. Almost ¾ mile (1.2km) after first joining the track, watch for a white pole and some boulders beside the path **D**. Turn sharp right here, heading downhill. When the track makes a decisive swing to the left, leave it by keeping straight ahead – through the middle of the field. Continue in the same direction beyond a dip, soon climbing again.

In the field's top corner, continue up to the gate **E** but don't go through it; instead, turn right on a fenced path along the airy ridge top. On reaching the Jockey Club gallops, keep straight ahead, soon joining a track. Follow this

Walking on the Lambourn Downs

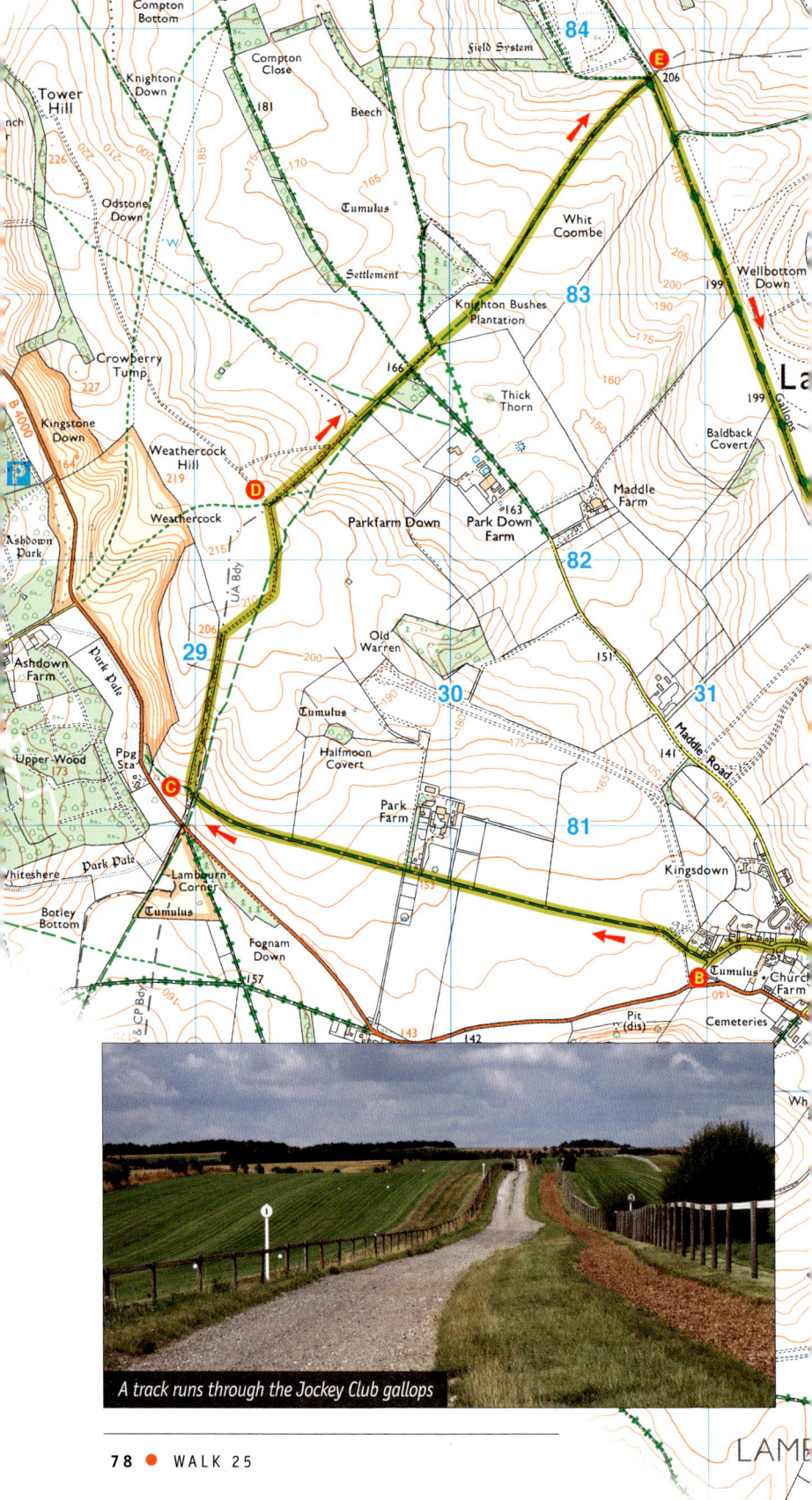

A track runs through the Jockey Club gallops

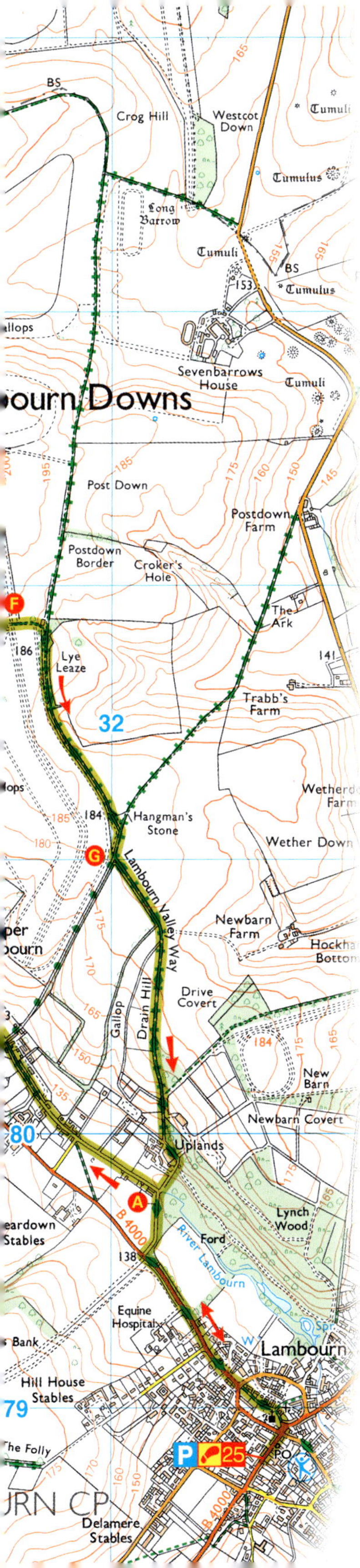

The Valley of the Racehorse

There are more than 1,500 racehorses based in and around Lambourn, making it the industry's second most important centre after Newmarket. The area has dozens of studs and training establishments, while the village itself hosts an equine hospital and a rehabilitation centre for injured jockeys. The link with racing dates from the 1730s when the Earl of Craven began holding meets near his family seat of Ashdown House.

for the next mile or so (1.9km). If you're lucky, there might be some racehorses being put through their paces – exciting both to see and hear. Reaching a vehicle track near a Jockey Club car park, cross diagonally left and carefully negotiate the gallops via the two white gates **F**. *Racehorses move fast, so you need to exercise caution.*

Join a surfaced track from the left. Immediately after a farm shed, turn left and quickly right along a shady byway. Step onto a vehicle track after a while, but only follow this for a few yards, soon bearing left to rejoin the more pleasant byway. Bear right at the next path junction. When the way ahead forks **G**, bear left along a rough lane. At the next split, go right. This lovely lane is known as Drain Hill.

At the first of the buildings at Uplands, follow the lane round to the left and then the right to the lane junction **A**. Retracing steps from earlier in the walk turn left along the B4000. When the road bends right, cross Big Lane to rejoin the paved path down the side of the church. Turn right at the market cross and go straight over at the crossroads. The car park is on the right in 125 yards.

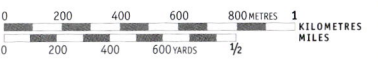

SCALE 1:25000 or 2½ INCHES to 1 MILE 4CM to 1KM

LAMBOURN DOWNS • 79

walk 26

Uffington White Horse and Wayland's Smithy

Start
Whitehorse Hill, near Uffington, Oxfordshire

Distance
8¾ miles (14.2km)

Height gain
720 feet (220m)

Approximate time
4¼ hours

Route terrain
Field paths; stony tracks; open pasture; short distance on surfaced lane

Parking
National Trust's Uffington White Horse car park (Pay and Display), 650 yards south of B4507 near Woolstone

Dog friendly
One awkward stile where dogs may need lifting **E**

OS maps
Landranger 174 (Newbury & Wantage), Explorer 170 (Vale of White Horse)

GPS waypoints
- SU 293 865
- **A** SU 301 862
- **B** SU 307 838
- **C** SU 292 822
- **D** SU 280 816
- **E** SU 278 822
- **F** SU 270 841
- **G** SU 281 853

There's a strong sense of stepping back in time as you explore the high ground above Uffington – a landscape that's been inhabited for millennia. Our ancestors have left their mark here. The White Horse itself, the fort of Uffington Castle and Wayland's Smithy are the obvious examples passed on this walk, but you'll come across lots of other mysterious lumps and bumps. Like many of the other North Wessex Downs routes in this book, this one includes a section along the Ridgeway.

There are several gates leading out on to the open hill from the far side of the car park. Take the one in the middle of the parking area, almost opposite the payment machine. Once through the gate, take the path heading east to the White Horse. It's difficult to get a good view of the chalk figure, other than from the air, but parts of it can be seen from here. After a gate, take the chalk path climbing on the far side of the road. At a signposted split, bear left. This trail passes over the top of the horse, fenced for protection. Immediately after the National Trust sign asking visitors to refrain from walking on the horse,

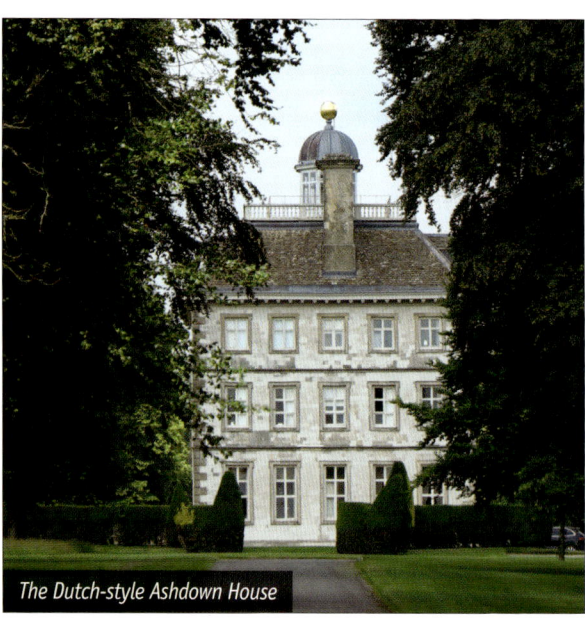

The Dutch-style Ashdown House

80 • WALK 26

turn right. The faint trail climbs towards the trig pillar on Whitehorse Hill (856 feet/261m). The trig pillar sits on the earthwork ramparts of Uffington Castle, an Iron Age hillfort. Swing slightly left and make for a gate **Ⓐ**. Once through this, turn right along the Ridgeway. In just a few yards, take the bridleway on the left – part of the Lambourn Valley Way. The route keeps to the right-hand edge of the field. At the far end, go left and immediately through the gap on the right – along a fenced strip beside the field.

In the next field, the footpath is marked out by lines of black-and-white posts. Stay between the posts. The route passes Idlebush Barrow, although there's not much to see on the ground. Just over 1½ miles (about 2.6km) after first joining the Lambourn Valley Way, abandon it as it passes round the side of a gate **Ⓑ**. Bear right after the gate – on a bridleway descending south-west through the field. Eventually, join a track continuing in roughly the same direction. At the top of a short but steep climb **Ⓒ**, keep straight ahead (west) on a trail through the middle of the field. After a gate on to access land, descend south-west. There's no path, although a faint trail might be discernible on dropping down the south side of the ridge. Come out at a kissing-gate. Cross the road and walk down the lane opposite. Ashdown House lies to the right in a short while.

The lane becomes a rough track. As it bends left, step forward to a gate straight ahead **Ⓓ**. Continue beyond the gate. At a bend in the track, keep right, following a footpath climbing beside the field boundary on the right. There's another glimpse of Ashdown House on the right on the ascent. Beyond a gate at the top of the rise, the earthwork remains of Alfred's Castle, an Iron Age settlement, can be seen on the left. After a stile **Ⓔ**, the temptation is to continue along the field edge, but swing slightly left (north-north-west). In

> **Wayland's Smithy** This elongated mound of chalk and earth was originally used as a burial site more than 5,500 years ago. The stone burial chamber itself has been reconstructed at one end of the mound, flanked by four massive, upright sarsen stones.

Wayland's Smithy

> **Ashdown House** This Dutch-style mansion was built by the first Earl of Craven in the late 17th century. He supposedly had it built for Elizabeth Stuart, the Queen of Bohemia, to whom he had been devoted for decades, but she died before it was completed. Access to the tenanted National Trust property is by pre-booked, guided tours on Wednesdays only.

spring and summer, these wildflower-filled meadows attract a vast range of butterflies.

After the next gate, keep heading in the same direction for about 30 yards and then, as a path heads right, along the woodland edge, veer slightly left, picking up a field path that quickly passes to the left of a few trees. This eventually leads out on to the Ridgeway **F**. Turn right along the broad, chalk track. About ¾ mile (1.3km) after crossing the road at Ashdown Hill, a trail on the left **G** leads to Wayland's Smithy – a detour of just 200 yards there and back, and well worth the effort. Continuing north on the Ridgeway, soon after crossing the next lane, the earthworks of Uffington Castle come into view ahead. At the next track crossing, turn left for Woolstone. Turn right along a surfaced lane and immediately go through the gate on the left. A faint trail through the grass roughly follows the line of the fence on the left, coming away from it slightly as it makes its way towards a fingerpost near some trees. On reaching this, go through the gates and drop down the steps to return to the car park. ●

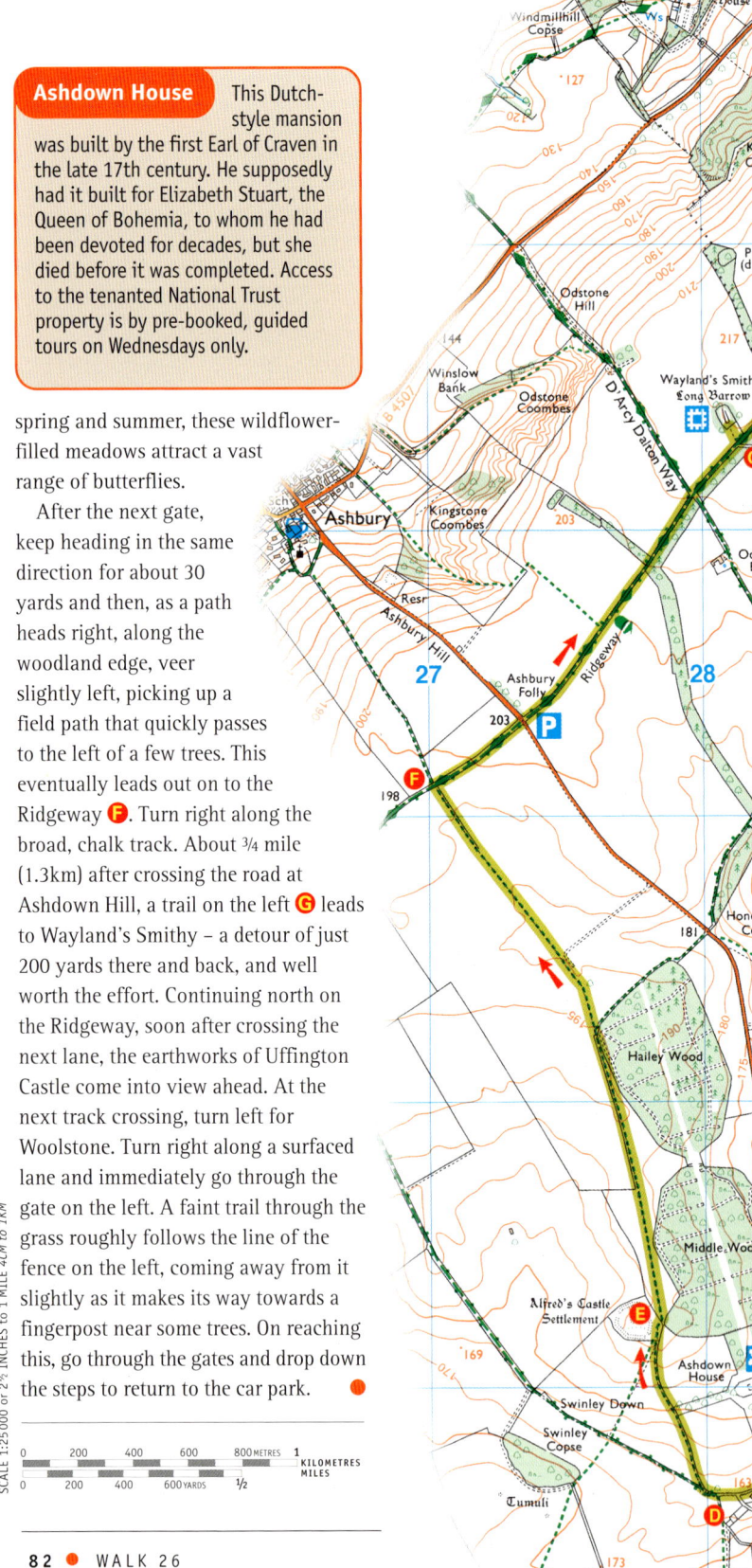

SCALE 1:25 000 or 2½ INCHES to 1 MILE 4CM to 1KM

82 ● WALK 26

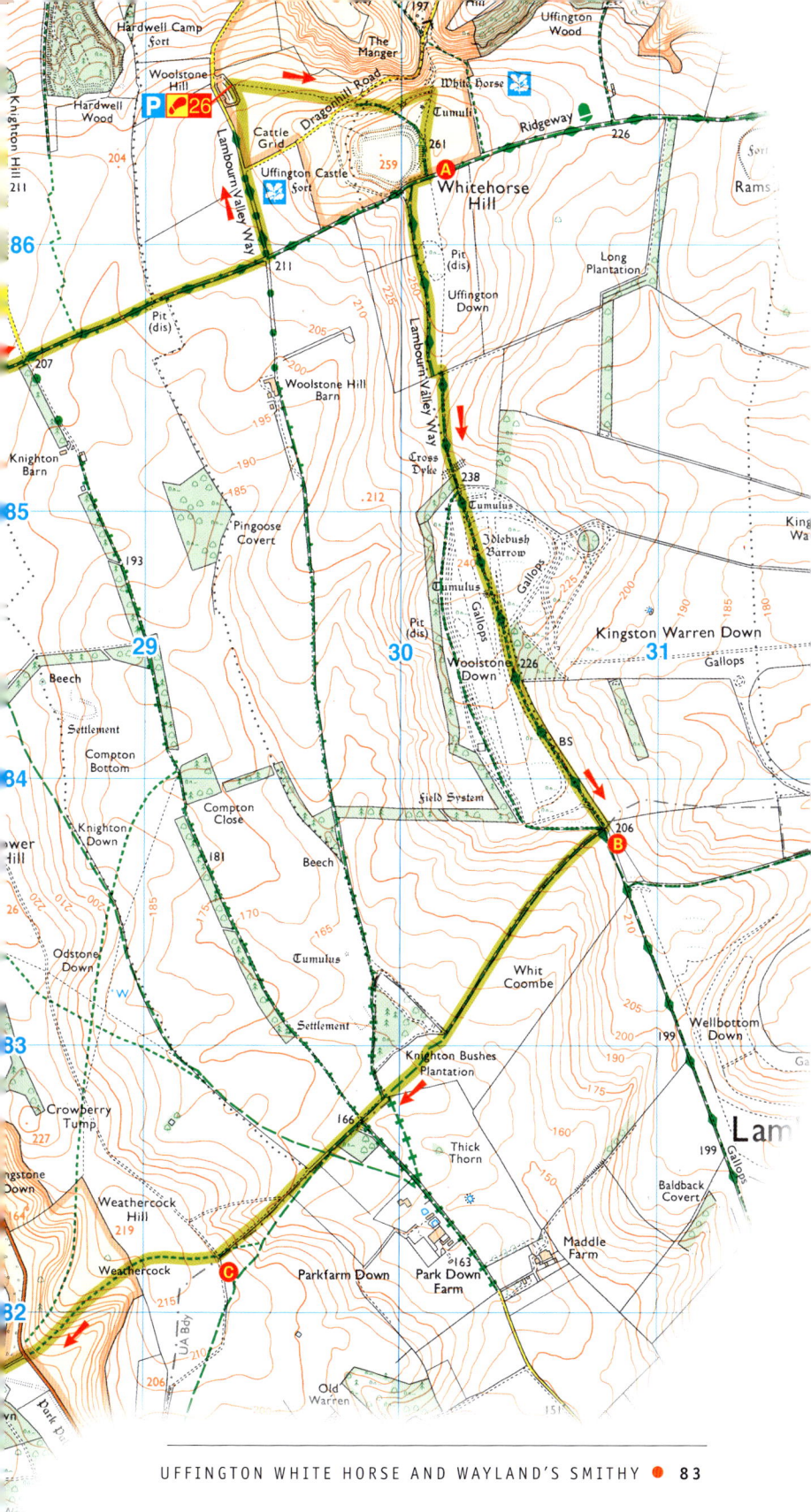

UFFINGTON WHITE HORSE AND WAYLAND'S SMITHY • 83

walk 27

River Lambourn and Donnington Castle

Start
Snelsmore Common, 1½ miles (2.4km) north of Donnington, Berkshire

Distance
9½ miles (15.3km)

Height gain
530 feet (160m)

Approximate time
4½ hours

Route terrain
Woodland trails; good tracks; some road walking; riverside paths; golf course

Parking
Snelsmore Common Country Park car park opposite toilet block and The Snugg; more parking beyond barriers

Dog friendly
Yes, but on leads on reserve during nesting season

OS maps
Landranger 174 (Newbury & Wantage), Explorer 158 (Newbury and Hungerford)

GPS waypoints
- SU 463 710
- **A** SU 458 707
- **B** SU 452 694
- **C** SU 442 701
- **D** SU 427 715
- **E** SU 437 701
- **F** SU 449 691
- **G** SU 460 685
- **H** SU 461 690

There's plenty of variety on this long and undulating walk through the Lambourn valley. It starts by heading through the tranquil woods and heathland of Snelsmore Common and then drops into the pretty village of Bagnor. An easy section on tracks and roads then leads to the thatched cottages of Boxford before a walk downstream with the River Lambourn. Nearing the end of the walk, a visit is paid to the hilltop tower of Donnington Castle before returning to Snelsmore Common.

Head into the woods, towards the alternative parking areas. Bear left as the lane splits beyond the barrier. Keep straight ahead through a gate – following an 'easy access' trail. Soon after this bends left, turn right along the signposted 'restricted byway'. Soon see a fire tower, once used to train firefighters, through the trees over on the left. Go straight over two path crossings. Beyond an open area, re-enter the trees. Immediately turn left **A**, heading downhill on the byway.

Go through a gate on the edge of the reserve and keep straight ahead. The path soon joins a vehicle track. When this bends right, keep straight on. The byway occupies a narrow strip of woodland as it passes through the Berkshire countryside. At the gates of a house, turn right along the signposted Lambourn Valley Way and then go right again at the road. Just after the road crosses Winterbourne Stream, The Watermill Theatre can be seen on the left. Take the next lane on the left **B**. Keep right at the gates to Bagnor Manor. Drawing level with a wooden gate on the left, turn right along a path between high hedges. After 450 yards, turn left. The route emerges from between the hedgerows at Copse Barn. Continue straight on until a large shed blocks the way. Go left here and then veer right – round the side of the shed – and on towards Bagnor Wood. As one path heads into the trees, keep right **C** – on a track skirting the beech wood.

When the track forks near the far end of Bagnor Wood, bear right. Now keep to the clearest track, tree-lined for much of the way, and follow it to the Winterbourne Road. Turn left along the asphalt and walk into Boxford. At a T-junction opposite some well-kept thatched cottages, turn left again. Opposite Mill House, go through the kissing-gate on the left **D** – rejoining

The ruins of Donnington Castle overlooking Newbury

the Lambourn Valley Way. Walk to the far end of this open area and through another metal kissing-gate.

The River Lambourn is followed downstream for some way now, although its presence may not always be detectable. In just more than a mile (about 1.8km) from the road in Boxford, there is a private track to the left. Immediately after this, bear left E, heading up into the trees. Beyond the woods, the route again passes between high hedgerows. Occasional gaps on the right provide lovely views over the Lambourn valley.

The route comes out on a track opposite Bagnor Manor, just a few yards from a point passed earlier in the walk. Turn sharp right – through a pedestrian gate next to a larger gate.

> **Donnington Castle** Not to be confused with Castle Donington in Leicestershire, this fortification was built in the late 14th century by Sir Richard Abberbury. All that remains today are some earthworks and the sturdy twin-towered gatehouse. Much of the structure was destroyed by Parliamentarians following several damaging attacks during the English Civil War.

RIVER LAMBOURN AND DONNINGTON CASTLE

The path leads to a bridge over the River Lambourn. Continue on a trail between two arms of the river. After a second bridge, follow the private driveway to a road and turn left. Walk along the asphalt for 250 yards and take the byway on the left. This can be muddy at times. About 350 yards from the road, go through the kissing-gate up to the right ❺ and turn sharp left along the field edge. Go through the next gate on the left. Continuing in roughly the same direction as before, bear right and follow this shady path along the edge of Rack Marsh nature reserve.

Turn right at the road and, in just a few strides, turn left along the Lambourn Valley Way. After passing under the A34, bear left at a fork in the path. Go straight over a track leading into a small industrial site. Turn right along a surfaced lane and immediately keep left as the lane splits. Pass in front of a gate and then take the path straight ahead, beside railings. Before long, the way resumes beside the river again, on the left, and a golf course on the right.

The right of way keeps close to the river, following a trail through the grass for 400 yards. Turn right across a more overgrown area and after a wooden footbridge ❻, bear left, passing just to the south of the pond but avoiding the surfaced golf buggy path. Turn left at a lane, keeping to the grass for now. Cross the white bridge over the river. Where the lane splits near a Donnington Grove Country Club sign, bear right and keep straight on at a crossing of routes. As the asphalt bends left, step off to the right. Pass to the right of a low hedge, ignoring the trail into the trees on the right. Immediately after this, the way ahead splits. Bear right and very soon see Donnington Castle up ahead.

Turn right to enter the castle's parking area and then go through the

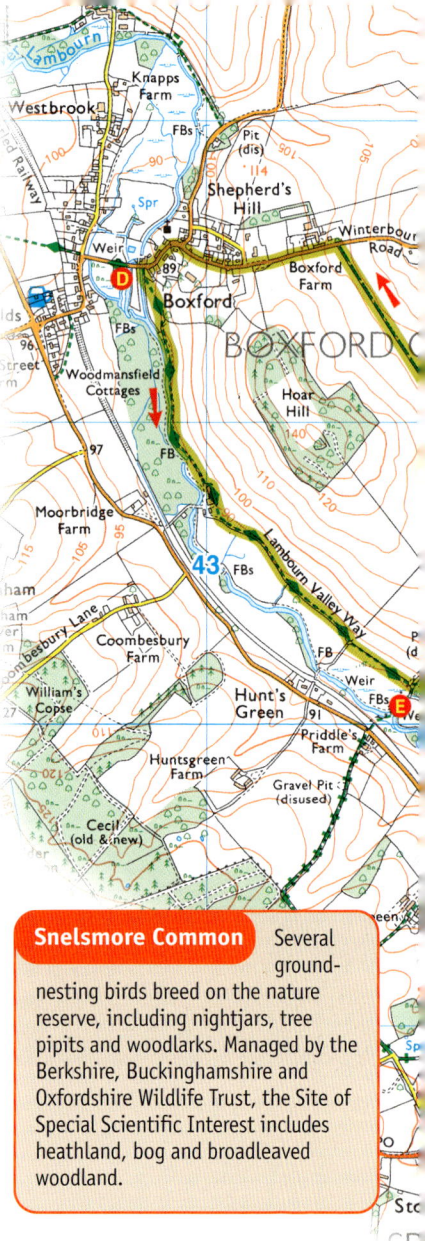

Snelsmore Common Several ground-nesting birds breed on the nature reserve, including nightjars, tree pipits and woodlarks. Managed by the Berkshire, Buckinghamshire and Oxfordshire Wildlife Trust, the Site of Special Scientific Interest includes heathland, bog and broadleaved woodland.

gate on the left to follow the path up to the tower ❼. You can't enter the ruins, but you can peer into them. It's a great spot to rest, occupying high ground with a good view of Newbury. As the path fades away, simply continue in the same direction, passing the castle on the left and dropping through a gate to leave the compound. Turn left along the rough lane. At a part-timbered house, turn left along a surfaced driveway, soon joining a lane from the left. After crossing the bridge over the A34, turn sharp right. (The 'no footpath' sign refers to the lane on the left.) At the next building, follow the bridleway to the left and re-enter the Snelsmore Common reserve. Keep straight ahead at all path crossings, seeing more of the reserve's open heathland than on the outward route. On reaching a T-junction with a restricted byway, turn right. Go through the second metal gate on the left to return to the parking area opposite the toilet block and **The Snugg** café.

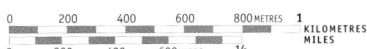

RIVER LAMBOURN AND DONNINGTON CASTLE ● 87

walk 28

Blenheim and beyond

🥾 **Start**	Woodstock, Oxfordshire
📏 **Distance**	10¼ miles (16.6km)
⛰ **Height gain**	700 feet (215m)
🕐 **Approximate time**	5 hours
👟 **Route terrain**	Pavement through town; parkland; farm tracks; field paths
🅿 **Parking**	Town centre car park on Hensington Road
🐕 **Dog friendly**	One awkward stile where dogs may need lifting Ⓐ; ladder stile between Ⓕ and Ⓖ
🧭 **OS maps**	Landranger 164 (Oxford), Explorer 180 (Oxford)
📍 **GPS waypoints**	
	SP 447 167
Ⓐ	SP 438 169
Ⓑ	SP 426 157
Ⓒ	SP 414 158
Ⓓ	SP 396 154
Ⓔ	SP 393 164
Ⓕ	SP 412 175
Ⓖ	SP 426 182

Starting from the popular Georgian town of Woodstock, this walk first heads out across the beautifully landscaped grounds of Blenheim Palace – beside The Lake, across parkland and through woods. The pretty village of Combe is visited before the route calls in at North Leigh Roman villa, home to an impressive mosaic floor dating from the fourth century AD. The River Evenlode is then crossed before walkers follow a Roman road across the fields back to Blenheim and then Woodstock.

Note that the route follows rights of way through the grounds of Blenheim Palace; other paths can be accessed by ticket-holders only.

> **Blenheim Palace** The seat of the Dukes of Marlborough and the home of the Spencer-Churchill family, this Unesco World Heritage Site was built in the early 18th century. It was designed in the Baroque style not by an architect but by a dramatist, Sir John Vanbrugh, who chose to include many grand and often extravagant features. The parkland and gardens seen today owe much of their majesty to the work of Capability Brown. The UK Prime Minister Sir Winston Churchill was born at Blenheim Palace in 1874.

Turn right out of the car park on to Hensington Road and go straight across the main road to walk down High Street. About 80 yards after passing St Mary Magdalene Church set back on the left, turn right along Chaucers Lane. At a sharp right bend, descend the steps to the main road and turn left. Just after a zebra crossing, go through the tall gates ahead, followed by a gate on the left leading into the grounds of Blenheim Palace. Turn right along the surfaced path and then take the next one on the left, quickly swinging back above the path just walked. About 175 yards along this path, cross the wooden stile in the electric fence on the right Ⓐ, and head uphill across the open parkland. There isn't a path on the ground; simply head south-west, passing about 125 yards left of the Column of Victory.

At a fence corner, bear left to walk with the fence on the right. At the next corner, come away from the fence to join a surfaced path via a gate. Turn left here and then go through the next pedestrian gate on the right. Drop to the side of The Lake. Walking with the water on the left, shortly pass Fair

The Column of Victory with Blenheim Palace behind

Rosamund's Well on the right. Climb the grassy path and then bear left along a clearer path, which enjoys particularly good views back towards the Grand Bridge.

At the far end of this western arm of The Lake, bear left at a fork. Go through the gate and swing right, walking beside the fence. Turn left along a surfaced track that passes through a gorgeous area of woodland, with some particularly grand old oaks. Just after a bench carved into a massive fallen tree trunk, bear right and go through a gate **B** to leave Blenheim's parkland. Turn right along the quiet road and take the next lane on the left – signposted Long Hanborough. After 250 yards, go through the gap in the wall on your right to join a footpath signposted 'Combe'. The route cuts straight across the field. Beyond a gap in the hedges, swing left and immediately right to walk downhill with the woods on the right. In a dip, bear right, through the trees and out into another field. Keep the woods on the right again until the woodland corner is reached. Now keep straight on, through the middle of the field. Once in the next field, the path makes directly for the church at Combe. Beyond a small patch of woodland, veer left along the edge of the recreational area and into the churchyard **C**.

Follow the path out through the gate and bear left along the walkway. Keep straight on along a red-and-black tiled pathway between the cottages and follow it to its conclusion. Now turn right along West End. At the next junction, turn left and then keep straight ahead, following a dead-end lane. At Higher Westfield Farm, pass between large sheds to the left and the farmhouse on the right, and then keep straight on, through a kissing-gate. A grassy track bends right. Cross the bridge over the River Evenlode and turn sharp left to follow it downstream. After a gate, a tunnel under the railway and a second gate, head straight across the meadow, away from the river. Beyond a kissing-gate, follow the field boundary uphill.

Half-way up the field, go through a kissing-gate **D** on the left. The substantial remains of North Leigh Roman Villa can be viewed on the left here. Turn sharp right and then right again along a track. About 150 yards after crossing a bridge over the railway, the track bends sharp right. Leave it here by going through the gate straight ahead. Now walk along the field edge and then drop to a waymarker post. Swing slightly right, later re-crossing the River Evenlode via a wooden footbridge **E**.

Take a few strides on the path straight ahead and then turn right through a kissing-gate. A grassy path runs parallel with the river for a few yards before swinging up to the left and going through another kissing-gate. Keep to the right-hand edge of two fields and then go straight across at the road, picking up the Oxfordshire Way. Once out in the field, maintain an almost straight line for 1 mile (1.6km) to the next road, walking with a field boundary on the left at first but later crossing to the other side. At the road 🅕, go straight over and continue in the same direction, with the hedgerow on the right again. Unsurprisingly, this dead-straight right of way follows the line of a Roman road – Akeman Street, which ran from St Albans to Cirencester. Cross the ladder stile over the Blenheim parkland wall and keep

The remains of North Leigh Roman villa

North Leigh Roman Villa

This large house would have been inhabited for about 300 years from the end of the first century AD. The small building on the far side of the site houses an impressive mosaic floor, a display of wealth by the family who lived in the villa. This is sometimes open to the public although it is also possible to view the tesserae through the window.

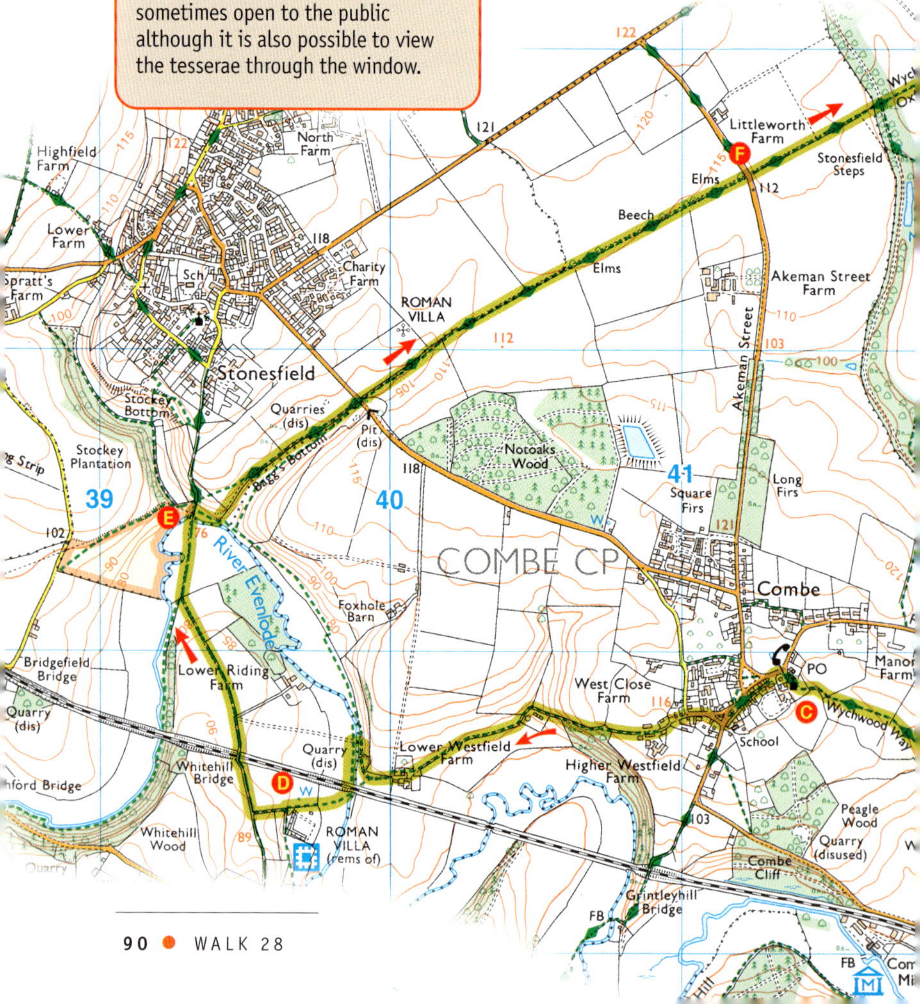

straight ahead, quickly leaving this strip of woodland via a gate. Continue on the same line as before, later crossing a surfaced lane to join a rough track. Cross a track junction, walking beside a fence.

Turn right along the next surfaced lane **G**. Blenheim's Column of Victory is immediately ahead now, with the Palace behind that. After a long straight stretch, follow the surfaced lane round to the left. Bear left when it forks. In another 500 yards, head left through the green gates where the parkland was entered earlier in the walk. Retrace outward steps back to the start of the walk.

BLENHEIM AND BEYOND

Further Information

Walking Safety

Although the reasonably gentle countryside that is the subject of this book offers no real dangers to walkers at any time of the year, it is still advisable to take sensible precautions and follow certain well-tried guidelines.

Always take with you both warm and waterproof clothing and sufficient food and drink. Wear suitable footwear, such as strong walking boots or shoes that give a good grip over stony ground, on slippery slopes and in muddy conditions. Try to obtain a local weather forecast and bear it in mind before you start. Do not be afraid to abandon your proposed route and return to your starting point in the event of a sudden and unexpected deterioration in the weather.

All the walks described in this book will be safe to do, given due care and respect, even during the winter. Indeed, a crisp, fine winter day often provides perfect walking conditions, with firm ground underfoot and a clarity unique to this time of the year. The most difficult hazard likely to be encountered is mud, especially when walking along woodland and field paths, farm tracks and bridleways – the latter in particular can often get churned up by cyclists and horses. In summer, an additional difficulty may be narrow and overgrown paths, particularly along the edges of cultivated fields. Always ensure appropriate footwear is worn.

Walkers and the Law

The Countryside and Rights of Way Act (CRoW Act 2000) gives a public right of access in England and Wales to land mapped as open country (mountain, moor, heath and down) or registered common land. These areas are known as *open access land*, and include land around the coastline, known as *coastal margin*.

Where You Can Go
Rights of Way
Prior to the introduction of the CRoW Act, walkers could only legally access the countryside along public rights of way. These are either 'footpaths' (for walkers only) or 'bridleways' (for walkers, riders on horseback and pedal cyclists). A third category called 'Byways open to all traffic' (BOATs), is used by motorised vehicles as well as those using non-mechanised transport. Mainly they are green lanes, farm and estate roads, although occasionally they will be found crossing mountainous area.

Rights of way are marked on Ordnance Survey maps. Look for the green broken lines on the Explorer maps, or the red dashed lines on Landranger maps.

The term 'right of way' means exactly what it says. It gives a right of passage over what, for the most part, is private land. Under pre-CRoW legislation walkers were required to keep to the line of the right of way and not stray on to land on either side. If you did inadvertently wander off the right of way, either because of faulty map reading or because the route was not clearly indicated on the ground, you were technically trespassing.

Local authorities have a legal obligation to ensure that rights of way are kept clear and free of obstruction, and are signposted where they leave metalled roads. The duty of local authorities to install signposts extends to the placing of signs along a path or way, but only where the authority considers it necessary to have a signpost or waymark to assist persons unfamiliar with the locality.

CRoW Access Rights
Access Land
As well as being able to walk on existing rights of way, under CRoW legislation you have access to large areas of open land and, under further legislation, a right of coastal access, which is being implemented by Natural England, giving for the first time the right of access around all England's

open coast. This includes plans for an England Coast Path (ECP) which will run for 2,795 miles (4,500 kilometres). A corresponding Wales Coast Path has been open since 2012.

Coastal access rights apply within the coastal margin (including along the ECP) unless the land falls into a category of excepted land or is subject to local restrictions, exclusions or diversions.

You can of course continue to use rights of way to cross access land, but you can lawfully leave the path and wander at will in these designated areas.

Where to Walk

Access Land is shown on Ordnance Survey Explorer maps by a light yellow tint surrounded by a pale orange border. New orange coloured 'i' symbols on the maps will show the location of permanent access information boards installed by the access authorities. Coastal Margin is shown on Ordnance Survey Explorer maps by a pink tint.

Restrictions

The right to walk on access land may lawfully be restricted by landowners, but whatever restrictions are put into place on access land they have no effect on existing rights of way, and you can continue to walk on them.

Dogs

Dogs can be taken on access land, but must be kept on leads of two metres or less between 1 March and 31 July, and at all times where they are near livestock. In addition landowners may impose a ban on all dogs from fields where lambing takes place for up to six weeks in any year. Dogs may be banned from moorland used for grouse shooting and breeding for up to five years.

General Obstructions

Obstructions can sometimes cause a problem on a walk and the most common of these is where the path across a field has been ploughed over. It is legal for a farmer to plough up a path provided that it is restored within two weeks. This does not always happen and you are faced with the dilemma of following the line of the path, even if this means treading on crops, or walking round the edge of the field. Although the latter course of action seems the most sensible, it does mean that you would be trespassing.

Other obstructions can vary from overhanging vegetation to wire fences across the path, locked gates or even a cattle feeder on the path.

Use common sense. If you can get round the obstruction without causing damage, do so. Otherwise only remove as much of the obstruction as is necessary to secure passage.

If the right of way is blocked and cannot be followed, there is a long-standing view that in such circumstances there is a right to deviate, but this cannot wholly be relied on. Although it is accepted in law that highways (and that includes rights of way) are for the public service, and if the usual track is impassable, it is for the general good that people should be entitled to pass into another line. However, this should not be taken as indicating a right to deviate whenever a way is impassable. If in doubt, retreat.

Report obstructions to the local authority and/or the Ramblers.

 Useful Organisations

Berkshire, Buckinghamshire and Oxfordshire Wildlife Trust
bbowt.org.uk

Campaign to Protect Rural England
15-21 Provost Street, London, N1 7NH
Tel. 020 7981 2800
cpre.org.uk

English Heritage
english-heritage.org.uk

Long Distance Walkers Association
ldwa.org.uk

Natural England
Tel. 0300 060 3900
gov.uk/government/organisations/natural-england

National Landscapes
national-landscapes.org.uk

National Trust
Membership and general enquiries:
Tel. 0344 800 1895
nationaltrust.org.uk
Berkshire, Buckinghamshire and Oxfordshire
Email: lse.customerenquiries:nationaltrust.org.uk

Ordnance Survey
ordnancesurvey.co.uk

Public transport
traveline.info
National Rail Enquiries
nationalrail.co.uk

Ramblers
13 Dirty Lane
London, SE1 9PA
Tel. 020 3961 3232
ramblers.org.uk

Rights of Way
West Berkshire Council
westberks.gov.uk/prow
Buckinghamshire Council
buckinghamshire.gov.uk/environment/countryside-and-public-rights-of-way/public-rights-of-way
Oxfordshire Council
oxfordshire.gov.uk/residents/environment-and-planning/countryside/countryside-access/public-rights-way

Tourist Information
Berkshire
visitingberkshire.uk
Buckinghamshire
visitsoutheastengland.com/places-to-visit/buckinghamshire
Oxfordshire
experienceoxfordshire.org

Youth Hostels Association
yha.org.uk

 Ordnance Survey maps for Berkshire, Buckinghamshire and Oxfordshire

The area of Berkshire, Buckinghamshire and Oxfordshire is covered by Ordnance Survey 1:50 000 (1¼ inches to 1 mile or 2cm to 1km) scale Landranger map sheets 151, 152, 163, 164, 165, 174 and 175. These all-purpose maps are packed with information to help you explore the area. Viewpoints, picnic sites, places of interest, and caravan and camping sites are shown, as well as public rights of way information such as footpaths and bridleways.

To examine the Berkshire, Buckinghamshire and Oxfordshire area in more detail and especially if you are planning walks, Ordnance Survey Explorer maps at 1:25 000 (2½ inches to 1 mile or 4cm to 1km) scale are ideal:

OL45 (The Cotswolds)
158 (Newbury & Hungerford)
160 (Windsor, Weybridge & Bracknell)
170 (Vale of White Horse)
171 (Chiltern Hills West)
172 (Chiltern Hills East)
180 (Oxford)
181 (Chiltern Hills North)
191 (Banbury, Bicester & Chipping Norton)
192 (Buckingham & Milton Keynes)

Text:	Vivienne Crow
Photography:	Vivienne Crow. Front cover: © travelib prime / Alamy Stock Photo
Editorial:	Ark Creative (UK) Ltd
Design:	Ark Creative (UK) Ltd

© Crown copyright / Ordnance Survey Limited, 2025
Published by Milestone Publishing Ltd under licence from Ordnance Survey Limited. Pathfinder, Ordnance Survey, OS and the OS logos are registered trademarks of Ordnance Survey Limited and are used under licence from Ordnance Survey Limited.
Text © Milestone Publishing Limited, 2025

This product includes mapping data licensed from Ordnance Survey
© Crown copyright and database rights (2025) OS AC0000819511

ISBN: 978-0-31909-227-9

While every care has been taken to ensure the accuracy of the route directions, the publishers cannot accept responsibility for errors or omissions, or for changes in details given. The countryside is not static: hedges and fences can be removed, field boundaries can alter, stiles can be replaced by gates, footpaths can be rerouted and changes in ownership can result in the closure or diversion of some concessionary paths. Also, paths that are easy and pleasant for walking in fine conditions may become slippery, muddy and difficult in wet weather, while stepping stones across rivers and streams may become impassable.

If you find an inaccuracy in either the text or maps, please contact Milestone Publishing at the address below.

First published 2022 by Milestone Publishing. Reprinted with amendments 2025.

Milestone Publishing, 18E Charles Street, Bath, BA1 1HX
pathfinderwalks.co.uk

Printed in India by Replika Press Pvt. Ltd. 2/25

GPSR Compliance: EU Authorised Representative: Easy Access System Europe - Mustamäe tee 50, 10621 Tallinn, Estonia. gpsr.requests@easproject.com

All rights reserved. No part of this publication may be reproduced, transmitted in any form or by any means, or stored in a retrieval system without either the prior written permission of the publisher, or in the case of reprographic reproduction a licence issued in accordance with the terms and licences issued by the CLA Ltd.

A catalogue record for this book is available from the British Library.

Front cover: Looking north from White Horse Hill, Uffington
Page 1: Walking across the farmland to the west of Chalgrove

Pathfinder® Guides — Britain's best-loved walking guides

Scotland
Pathfinder Walks
- 3 ISLE OF SKYE
- 4 CAIRNGORMS
- 7 FORT WILLIAM & GLEN COE
- 19 DUMFRIES & GALLOWAY
- 23 LOCH LOMOND, THE TROSSACHS, & STIRLING
- 27 PERTHSHIRE, ANGUS & FIFE
- 30 LOCH NESS & INVERNESS
- 31 OBAN, MULL & KINTYRE
- 46 ABERDEEN & ROYAL DEESIDE
- 47 EDINBURGH, PENTLANDS & LOTHIANS
- 82 ORKNEY & SHETLAND
- 83 NORTH COAST 500 & NORTHERN HIGHLANDS
- 85 OUTER HEBRIDES
- 88 SCOTTISH BORDERS

North of England
Pathfinder Walks
- 15 YORKSHIRE DALES
- 22 MORE LAKE DISTRICT
- 28 NORTH YORK MOORS
- 39 DURHAM, NORTH PENNINES & TYNE AND WEAR
- 42 CHESHIRE
- 49 VALE OF YORK & YORKSHIRE WOLDS
- 53 LANCASHIRE
- 60 LAKE DISTRICT
- 63 PEAK DISTRICT
- 64 SOUTH PENNINES
- 71 THE HIGH FELLS OF LAKELAND
- 73 MORE PEAK DISTRICT
- 86 LAKE DISTRICT & CUMBRIA ACCESSIBLE WALKS
- 87 NORTHUMBERLAND
- 93 NORTH YORKSHIRE ACCESSIBLE WALKS

Wales
Pathfinder Walks
- 10 ERYRI/SNOWDONIA
- 18 BRECON BEACONS
- 34 PEMBROKESHIRE & CARMARTHENSHIRE
- 41 MID WALES
- 55 GOWER, SWANSEA & CARDIFF
- 78 ANGLESEY, LLEYN & ERYRI/SNOWDONIA
- 79 DEE VALLEY, CLWYDIAN HILLS & NORTH EAST WALES

Heart of England
Pathfinder Walks
- 6 COTSWOLDS
- 20 SHERWOOD FOREST & THE EAST MIDLANDS
- 29 WYE VALLEY & FOREST OF DEAN
- 74 THE MALVERNS TO WARWICKSHIRE
- 80 SHROPSHIRE
- 81 STAFFORDSHIRE
- 84 BERKSHIRE, BUCKINGHAMSHIRE & OXFORDSHIRE

East of England
Pathfinder Walks
- 44 ESSEX
- 45 NORFOLK
- 48 SUFFOLK
- 50 LINCOLNSHIRE & THE WOLDS
- 51 CAMBRIDGESHIRE & THE FENS

South West of England
Pathfinder Walks
- 1 SOUTH DEVON & DARTMOOR
- 5 CORNWALL
- 9 EXMOOR & THE QUANTOCKS
- 11 DORSET & THE JURASSIC COAST
- 26 DARTMOOR
- 68 NORTH & MID DEVON
- 69 SOUTH WEST ENGLAND'S COAST
- 76 SOMERSET & THE MENDIPS
- 77 WILTSHIRE

South East of England
Pathfinder Walks
- 8 KENT
- 12 NEW FOREST, HAMPSHIRE & SOUTH DOWNS
- 25 THAMES VALLEY & CHILTERNS
- 54 HERTFORDSHIRE & BEDFORDSHIRE
- 65 SURREY
- 66 SOUTH DOWNS NATIONAL PARK & WEST SUSSEX
- 67 SOUTH DOWNS NATIONAL PARK & EAST SUSSEX
- 72 THE HOME COUNTIES FROM LONDON BY TRAIN
- 94 ISLE OF WIGHT

Practical Guide
- 75 NAVIGATION SKILLS FOR WALKERS

City Walks
- LONDON
- OXFORD
- EDINBURGH